Critical Praise for the New-Generation African Poets Chapbook Box Set Series

"Dawes and Abani have taken on the vital project of publishing short collections by contemporary poets from Africa, packaged together in beautiful boxed sets." —*New York Times Magazine*

"An ambitious, vital project that delivers exactly what it promises... As a group, the chapbooks dispel stereotypes about African writing. They also illustrate what editors Dawes and Abani note about the many ways poets can understand or redefine their ties to Africa. These insights are poignant and valuable, especially at a time when millions around the globe find themselves somewhere between new countries and ancestral lands they've left behind." —*Washington Post*

"Editors Dawes and Abani introduce readers to eleven emerging African poets with distinctive perspectives in this twelve-piece, limited-edition box set. Sponsored by the African Poetry Book Fund (APBF), this project has been in production since 2014." —*Ebony*

"The African Poetry Book Fund's New-Generation African Poets: A Chapbook Box Set series is one of the most important annual literary projects, presenting to a wide audience the work of fresh and promising poets in the continent and its diaspora." —*Open Country*

"We live in a curated world; the beauty of this collection is not just in the interplay of cover art and text, of preface and poem, but especially in its overall optimistic effect. This isn't a curatorial project solely focused on refining our world, cutting it down to manageable size, reflecting the literary interests of its editors. Though it does this, it simultaneously opens up a whole new emergent modern trajectory of African poetry, adding to it words that are surprising not in their existence—we know that with greater funding, similar projects, changing patterns of readership, more than eight, more than ten new African poetry chapbooks of this quality could reach us each year—but in their specific, trenchant voices. Start clearing off a set of shelves—this is something to make space for, year after year." —*Africa in Words*

TOWARD A LIVING ARCHIVE OF AFRICAN POETRY

Kwame Dawes and Chris Abani on the
New-Generation African Poets Chapbook Series

EDITED AND WITH A FOREWORD BY
Siwar Masannat

No part of this book may be reproduced, stored in a retrieval system, or transmitted in any form, by any means, including mechanical, electronic, photocopying, recording, or otherwise, without the prior written consent of the publisher.

Published by Akashic Books
©2025 Kwame Dawes and Chris Abani
Foreword ©2025 Siwar Masannat

ISBN: 978-1-63614-255-5
Library of Congress Control Number: 2024951174

All rights reserved
First printing

EU Authorized Representative details:
Easy Access System Europe
Mustamäe tee 50, 10621 Tallinn, Estonia
gpsr.request@easproject.com

Akashic Books
Brooklyn, New York
Instagram, X, Facebook:
AkashicBooks
info@akashicbooks.com
www.akashicbooks.com

African Poetry Book Fund
Brown University
10 Prospect Street
Box A
Providence, RI 02912
apbf@brown.edu

*For Lorna,
Sena, Kekeli, Akua,
Mama the Great,
and the tribe: Gwyneth, Kojo, Adjoa, and Kojovi.
Remembering Aba and Neville.
K.D.*

*

*Remembering Daphne, Michael, and Greg;
and for Mark, Charles, and Stella—my family.
I love you.
C.A.*

AFRICAN POETRY BOOK SERIES

SERIES EDITOR
Kwame Dawes

EDITORIAL BOARD
Chris Abani, Northwestern University
Gabeba Baderoon, Pennsylvania State University
Kwame Dawes, Brown University
Phillippa Yaa de Villiers, University of the Witwatersrand
Bernardine Evaristo, Brunel University of London
Aracelis Girmay, Stanford University
John Keene, Rutgers University–Newark
Matthew Shenoda, Brown University

ADVISORY BOARD
Glenna Luschei
Elizabeth Alexander
Sulaiman Adebowale

CONTENTS

Foreword by Siwar Masannat   9

Introduction to   19
Seven New-Generation African Poets
2014

Introduction to   29
Eight New-Generation African Poets: A Chapbook Box Set
2015

Introduction to   37
Tatu: New-Generation African Poets, A Chapbook Box Set
2016

Introduction to   49
Nne: New-Generation African Poets, A Chapbook Box Set
2017

Introduction to   61
Tano: New-Generation African Poets, A Chapbook Box Set
2018

Introduction to   71
Sita: New-Generation African Poets, A Chapbook Box Set
2019

Introduction to   91
Saba: New-Generation African Poets, A Chapbook Box Set
2020

Introduction to   119
Nane: New-Generation African Poets, A Chapbook Box Set
2021

Introduction to   133
Tisa: New-Generation African Poets, A Chapbook Box Set
2023

Introduction to   143
Kumi: New-Generation African Poets, A Chapbook Box Set
2024

"THE PROMISE OF BEING SEEN":
Gestures in Kwame Dawes and Chris Abani's Curation of Emerging African Poetry
BY SIWAR MASANNAT

Collected here in your hands are Kwame Dawes and Chris Abani's introductory essays for the New-Generation African Poets series. These essays are conversations that celebrate the work of emerging African poets and build—meticulously and with principled care—a vision of a pluralistic literary community in which poets may thrive. For more than ten years, Dawes and Abani have offered readers a glimpse into their editorial labor and philosophy, which are guided by generosity, curiosity, and trust in the work of African poets. These essays historicize the need for the work of the African Poetry Book Fund (APBF), locating its effort in relation to a gap in the publishing landscape, where African fiction has historically received far more attention than poetry, and where African poets, both on the continent and in the diaspora, do not typically enjoy access to literary establishments that nurture their work. Dawes and Abani's editorial labor is a gift, an expansive curation that honors the past, present, and future of African poetry.

In 2024, the APBF celebrated the publication of the tenth box set in the New-Generation African Poets series. Each of the box sets, edited by Dawes and Abani, features a selection of chapbooks by emerging African authors who have not yet published a full-length collection of poetry. Publishing these chapbooks is a community effort. On its website, the APBF makes transparent the selection process. Recommendations from editors, board members, and authors associated with the APBF, as well as manuscripts received through the Evaristo Prize for African Poetry (previously the Brunel International African Poetry Prize) and the Sillerman First Book Prize for African Poetry, shape a list of emerging poets of note. The APBF then writes to the poets, inviting them to submit a manuscript for Dawes and Abani's consideration.

With a design conceptualized as a "moveable gallery," the box sets are striking artistic objects: the box and each of the chapbook covers feature artwork by a single African visual artist. The first box set in the series, published by Slapering Hol Press in 2014, featured eight pieces of art by Adejoke Tugbiyele (Nigeria). TJ Dema (Botswana), Clifton Gachagua (Kenya), Tsitsi Jaji (Zimbabwe), Nick Makoha (Uganda), Ladan Osman (Somalia), Warsan Shire (Somalia/Kenya), and Len Verwey (South Africa) were the first "new-generation" poets to be published in the series. Nine subsequent box sets, each featuring between eight and thirteen emerging African poets, were published by the APBF in collaboration with Akashic Books. To date, Dawes and Abani have edited eighty-nine chapbooks by poets from twenty-four countries and all regions of Africa and its diasporas. Many of the poets have gone on to publish full-length collections, win prestigious awards, and contribute to a thriving African poetic landscape across the globe. Also important to note is one of the generous choices made by the editors in the execution of this series: each chapbook opens with a preface, written by an established poet, that offers a critical discussion and celebration of the work. The emerging authors, therefore, encounter their poetic achievement as one that is already embedded in creative community, embraced by peers and literary elders alike.

Often, the essays collected here seek to (re)position African poetry and its reception without foreclosing what constitutes an African poetic. At a time when problematic imaginaries continue to consolidate reductive and binary-based frameworks in relation to peoples, cultures, belongings, and migration, Dawes and Abani repeatedly affirm their commitment to an expansive Africanness and a broad range of aesthetics. The editors chart a set of guiding beliefs, open questions, and curatorial practices that elucidate their intervention in the publishing landscape and the transnational nature of the body of literature circulating via the APBF. The chapbooks emerge from and are received by numerous literary environments, be they on the African continent or in the African diaspora across the US and world. As such, Dawes and Abani often address multiple audiences in their essays, audiences whose aesthetic tastes, analytical frameworks, and lived experiences may be as incommensurable as they are shared. They do not speak from a presumed center to a periphery, as many editors in Western publishing markets are inclined to do, mining "other" literatures based on provincial and impoverished imperial imaginaries. Rather, Dawes and Abani address audiences from the recognition of their editorial position as part of a growing network of alive and interrelated cultural locations. In other words, they are in conversation by way of participating in (and sustaining) a heterogeneous community.

Dawes and Abani's essays are organized in movements that work in concert and symbiosis, and, when read together, offer readers the pleasure of observing their reflexive and recursive thinking. They return to themes and arguments that appear in earlier essays; they pick up kernels of future plans and reflect on their progress or further build on them. They might offer additional context for the other's movement, or an interpretation of one of his arguments, or they might respond to one another's prompts. Holding poetry at the center, Dawes and Abani enact—critically and editorially—the motions that they identify in the poetry itself.

One of the most striking gestures in these essays is their storytelling. Both Dawes and Abani use anecdotes as entry points into engaging with a real, embodied community. Anecdotes serve as organic, situated ways to trace a point of origin, identify heterogeneity and complexity in creative practice, intervene in problematic trends of reception, or respond to community feedback. For instance, in the introduction to the first box set, *Seven New-Generation African Poets*, Abani recalls how Dawes cofounded the Afro-Style School of Poetics in London to counteract the exclusion of Black writers in the literary milieu, marking a moment of community engagement and leadership amongst only a handful of other organizations founded by Black poets at the time (23). In another anecdote, Dawes recalls a dialogue between an elder poet and emerging poet in Nigeria regarding questions of poetic tradition—an incident that launches a larger, important conversation about cultural authenticity, literary legacy, innovation, and choice of language in African poetics (71–72). The exchange demonstrates beautifully how Dawes and Abani afford African poetics polyvocal, rich regard.

Another gesture that may be glimpsed across these essays is pedagogical. For instance, some of the essays offer encouragement to critics who might wish to engage the nuances of African poetics. Consider the ways Dawes and Abani respond to cultural frames and polemics. Part of this pedagogical penchant also works as a corrective to mainstream publishers in the US, such as in Dawes's attempt to problematize condescending narratives of discovery (50). Yet another real and imagined audience of these pedagogical gestures is African poets. In centering the poets' artistry, Dawes and Abani affirm the work of the emerging generation and treat it with respect and seriousness. The editors reflect the poets' work back to them with care, embedding the "new generation" in established and ever-transforming African and global literary contexts. At the same time, they are careful not to foreclose the space of creative engagement, offering subtle, non-prescriptive guidance in the form of observations and open questions, in an implicit invitation to practice writing poetry that does not align with trends.

I am interested in the distinct styles in which Dawes and Abani discuss African poetics, and the convergence of their observations and arguments, which move in productive, evocative directions. Dawes often emphasizes voice, genius, and urgency in poetic expression. He observes the emergence of an African "lyric self" as a heuristic for critically engaging with poetry. This heuristic first appears in response to the anecdote I mentioned earlier, when an elder Nigerian author asserts that younger generations have eschewed African traditions. While acknowledging these intergenerational anxieties, as well as the material conditions that have created linguistic and cultural ruptures for younger generations, Dawes locates emerging African poets' concern with their roots in their explorations of family and belonging. This points to a "persistent sense that . . . [contemporary poets] engage the past in the manner of the lyric self" (83). He thus expands the legibility of tradition from a static conception of Africanness toward an individual exploration of lineage and experience. In turn, Abani problematizes the implications of "legacy." Charting the history of gendered access to writing systems, he notes the heteropatriarchal consolidation of tradition and the exclusion of women's literature from African cultural legacies. By turning away from legacy as a "noun," Abani emphasizes the editors' interest in "living literature, in a living archive, in the verb of legacy" (89).

Dawes subsequently returns to the lyric self to parse how poets engage with the border as a permeable boundary and a site fraught with historical and contemporary power dynamics. In a movement titled "*Sankofa*," he offers a beautiful interpretation of the chapbooks in the *Saba* box set to demonstrate how poets

> are negotiating, in the most sophisticated and revealing ways, themes of place, history, and transition . . . Borders are the sites of war, of escape, of discovery, of ethnic divisions, and more hopefully, the sites of imagination remaking, of cross-fertilization, of the strange confluence of cultures and ideas and bodies. (95)

The connections that Dawes builds between the lyric self and the border trouble the boundary between the personal and political, expanding how we conceive of the individual's poetic voice. In his introduction to *Saba*, Abani explains Dawes's suggestive title, offering a wonderful linguistic meditation on the Akan word *Sankofa*. Describing West African conceptions of language as a vehicle for implying complex experience, he writes, "What we encounter here, is a return to that much more complex and advanced philosophy of self that the African past offers" (115). With these critical gestures, Dawes and Abani not only validate the power of younger poets, but co-create a culturally specific framework for interpreting their work.

Whereas Dawes often arrives at the transnational aspect of African poetry via an emphasis on the lyric self as a heuristic, Abani often begins by tracing the broad poetic inclinations exhibited by literary movements of the twentieth and twenty-first centuries. For instance, he offers a critique of the "early rush to nationalism" in the continent's postcolonial past, noting that nation-building at times stifled poetry (34). He identifies contemporary poets' work as taking up what the building of nation-states "interrupted" (34) and going beyond the oppositional stance of the Negritude movement, which conceived of African art as "expressions of the soul that stand against and in opposition to Western forms of the mind" (45). While Abani implicitly suggests a post-national orientation for contemporary poets—one that straddles the global and local without being beholden to predetermined national modes of expression—he is careful to highlight how poets "attempt a continental and global self that is expansive enough to flow like the Niger but never loses the nation that birthed it" (25). Abani pronounces this complex poetic orientation and motion as made possible through the constitution of the lyric self.

Another enlightening thread of Dawes and Abani's conversation on African poetics is the question of language(s). The editors acknowledge the fact that Anglophone publishing is limited by language, considering the vast multilingualism of the African continent. That said, they articulate language choice not merely as a personal preference, but more precisely as it emerges in relation to the material conditions which shape access, education, translation, and literary circulation. Moreover, they celebrate the heterogeneity and multilingualism of the continent's literary lineages by problematizing absolute separations between colonial and indigenous languages, thus challenging the notion that the choice of English as a poetic language undermines the authenticity or Africanness of the work. For instance, Dawes and Abani describe the process of "derivation" as a creative practice quite distinct from the "derivative" as a pejorative notion, recognizing African Englishes as "artistic interventions, innovations, endlessly expanding, within the system of English but with permeable borders" (125). In his essay "The Horse of Language," Abani turns to the metaphor of journey-making to parse out the African philosophies that influence linguistic practice in the work of emerging poets (110). Abani beautifully articulates the centrality of the journey to poetic expression, demonstrating the layers of multidimensional motion in African thought. This concept evokes the work of scholars such as Azade Seyhan, Walter Mignolo, and Gerald Vizenor, who have written about linguistic innovations that elude commodification.

Many thought-provoking threads related to African poetics appear across the essays. One is Abani's concept of a "living archive" (89). Another is Dawes and Abani's challenge to the hierarchical values ascribed to oral and written literature within colonial conceptions. They complicate the dichotomy between oral and written, and triangulate African poetic lineages by linking continental spoken word poetry, Caribbean reggae, and African American hip-hop aesthetics to the written word. I will not rehash all the wonderful anecdotes, observations, and arguments that Dawes and Abani so generously share in these essays, as they are best encountered by readers through the editors' own words.

To close, I would like to mention what I find to be the most compelling gesture of all, which is Dawes and Abani's nurturing of community. As they explain, the APBF's editorial work arises from community and is intended to cultivate and broaden a sense of recognition and belonging amongst African poets. First and foremost, the role of the APBF as a literary organization releases African poets from the commodifying and exoticizing market demands of Western publishing, opening up a space for their poetry to speak on its own terms. From historicizing the publication of African poetry in the Heinemann African Writers Series, to identifying the practical challenges facing the global circulation of poetry books, Dawes and Abani situate the APBF's effort as community-based—an effort that builds on the past and relies on a growing network of readers and writers of African poetry. As such, they advance a transnational vision for African poetry. Their literary leadership helps to imagine and create a landscape in which the work of as many poets as possible can thrive, receive recognition, and be preserved for future generations. For, as they say in their introduction to *Nane*, "the idea of a poetic community enacts the promise of being seen" (121).

—Siwar Masannat
April 2025

INTRODUCTION TO
SEVEN NEW-GENERATION AFRICAN POETS
2014

Featured poets: TJ Dema, Clifton Gachagua, Tsitsi Jaji, Nick Makoha, Ladan Osman, Warsan Shire, Len Verwey

Featured artist: Adejoke Tugbiyele

Introduction in Two Movements

Part One

Recently, an American of fairly immediate Nigerian heritage (he was born in the United States to Nigerian immigrants) won the Caine Prize. As expected, there was a bit of a tempest about this. The Caine Prize, after all, prides itself on having a strong reach into Africa and discovering previously hidden African talent in fiction. Was this the kind of writer that the Caine Prize was established to benefit?

Those who say "no" mean that the writer, as an American, has full access to publishing opportunities in the United States, to training as a writer, and to a lively literary scene. Because they have no such opportunities, Africans who live in Africa are less easily found. The mandates of the Caine Prize, the BBC Short Story Prize, the Brunel University African Poetry Prize, and now the Sillerman First Book Prize for African Poets, all claim to offer such opportunities to African writers in Africa.

Yet not everyone makes residence in Africa a contest requirement. The reason is uncomplicated: Africans, like everyone else in this migration-crazy world, move. Those who move are not just the wealthy and privileged. When they move, the circumstances that make it difficult for them to succeed as writers in Africa are not automatically erased. This is because of the troubling nature of African poetry and fiction. One might develop a narrow idea of a body of work on nationalistic terms, but continental labels become complicated. When does a Nigerian stop being a Nigerian and become an African American? The Caine Prize and the Brunel University African Poetry Prize have both estimated that after one generation, the burden of nationalism ends.

As we thought about the African Poetry Book Fund (APBF) Series, these issues were raised and discussed. We chose to focus on the core reason for the establishment of the fund in the first place. It guided us. We established the fund to fill a gap. Until the African Poetry Book Fund was established, one was hard-pressed to find a publisher devoted exclusively to the publishing of poetry from Africa. We decided to change that with a simple but effective plan: four books a year, a series of partnerships, an African base, a U.S. base, and a network of associations to make this work happen. With the generosity of Laura and Robert F. X. Sillerman, who gave us the significant seed money, guidance, support, and encouragement, and who continue to be our main benefactors, along with the generous contributions from other folks who have come to share the vision for this work and, beyond that, the commitment, generosity, and passion of the volunteer team of editors—each one a prime mover and shaker in his or her own right—we have created an exciting collaboration.

This chapbook box set came about because we saw great talent in the work submitted for the Sillerman First Book Prize for African Poets, and we wanted to find a way to expose the world to that work. We found three especially dynamic poets in that pool; and then through a series of inquiries to some of the writers, publishers, and arts programmers around the world, we invited a select group of poets to submit work for consideration. The material was electrifying—contemporary, urgent, urbane, lively, and marked by innovative craft—and so, after much deliberation, we settled on four other poets. In one fell swoop, we had amassed a collection of new generation African poetry!

When the Poetry Foundation's Ilya Kaminsky approached me about putting together an anthology of new African poetry, the chapbook box set seemed like an inspired compromise; and this began the extensive period of scouting, meeting, pitching, and regrouping to find a press in the United States to gather with us on this unusual chapbook series. Even before we had a partner squared away, Chris Abani and I worked assiduously with the poets to make their collections ready for publication. We came very close in negotiations with four poetry presses, but for a variety of reasons, not the least of which was the catch-22 of "we have never done this before, nobody has, so we have no model for it, and so we have to pass," they balked. Our timeline did not help matters either—we were working for a 2014 release date—and beyond that, our budget was limited. We were, however, encouraged by the enthusiasm that each of the publishers showed in reaction to the concept and to the work.

At a breakfast meeting in New York City, Laura Sillerman proposed Slapering Hol Press (SHP), the small press imprint of The Hudson Valley Writers' Center, that she had learned about at the 2013 Association of Writers and Writing Programs (AWP)

Conference. I contacted SHP's founding Editor, Margo Taft Stever, and her prompt and enthusiastic interest was encouraging. The existence of the box set today says a great deal about the value of vision, commitment, and partnership that has had to operate over the last ten months to publish this important set of literary collections. Despite the challenges, we are committed to publishing a box set of chapbooks by new African poets. Our basic plan will remain the same: to give each of our poets one hundred copies of their respective chapbooks. We will continue to invite gifted African artists to have their work featured in a box set—a veritable moveable gallery—and to employ multiple approaches to invite poets to be considered for this collection.

But for all the ins and outs of putting this box set together, for all the fundraising, the partnerships forged, and the extensive negotiations concerning the project, ultimately this box set exists because of the talent and urgency of these poems. The work demanded that we find a way to publish it and to make it available to our readers. These volumes, which are original, are as diverse in thematic concerns, poetic styles, and musicality as the peoples of Africa and its diaspora. They are books of poetry that reveal a complex and sophisticated awareness of the world. Of the seven poets collected here, three live in African countries (Kenya, Botswana, and South Africa) and four live outside of Africa (Jaji and Osman in the United States and Makoha and Shire in the United Kingdom). Yet they all self-identify as Africans in the full and complicated way that Africanness is best defined.

Ultimately, the poems manage to chart in rich and textured ways the idea of Africa in our contemporary space. We are finding in these poets a cadre of writers who remain committed to the rich and enduring challenge of finding a voice and idiom that manages to reflect a quality of modernity operating in African cultures. We are far less interested in the question of legitimizing a certain kind of Africanness than we are in allowing the art itself to offer us ways to see and engage with what it all means. These poets are haunted by the compulsion to make art, to use language to chart their realities in verse. We are the beneficiaries of their efforts.

—Kwame Dawes
Lincoln, Nebraska

Part Two

The conversations that led to this African Poetry Book Fund initiative began years ago in London without any of the parties now involved understanding where that conversation was going. In 1996, Kwame Dawes set up the Afro-Style School of Poetics, came to London, and began to teach workshops to a gaggle of young black poets, including Bernardine Evaristo, who is on the APBF editorial board and one of the most important black poets working today, and me.

Dawes's vision was simple: He identified a gap in the publishing of young black poets (African, Caribbean, and Indian writers—in England in those days, black was as much a political identity as it was racial or ethnic) and sought a way to close it. He thought if we were given the same instruction and mentoring as our white contemporaries, we would close the gap on our own. Evaristo, at the time, ran a literary organization called Spread the Word, which helped target and implement the Afro-Style School. But it was Dawes, himself part Jamaican and part Ghanaian, after winning the Forward Prize and poised on the edge of bigness, as we say, who reached back to make sure his ascent was not singular. And so it happens in the way all secular Rasta ting happen—one are lead the way and rest are just follow out of Babylon. Seen. Perhaps it was in the water then; this was the time of Soul ii Soul and other such amalgamations of arts and the politics of blackness. As our Fada Linton Kwesi Johnson put it, "righteous, righteous war!"

But the thing is, the Afro-Style School and Kwame Dawes were the beating heart of a certain change. Nearly everyone who was in those workshops has gone on to have a gloriously published career—the two already mentioned, Roger Robinson, Akure Wall, Dorothea Smart, Kadija Sesay, Raman Mundair, Karen McCarthy, and Malika Booker, to name a few. His mentorship has continued for almost two decades and now includes poets like Nick Makoha, who is one of the poets featured in this box set.

So in the way all things do, it circles back to Africa—the Poetry Africa road tour of 2011, to be specific, curated by that little-sung hero of African arts Peter Rorvrik (and his remarkable team led by the inimitable Maggy Reddy). Kwame Dawes, Shailja Patel, Khadijatou Doynel, Didier Awadi, T-bass, Gabeba Gaberoon (also on the APBF editorial board), TJ Dema, the magnificent Lebo Mashile, and I toured through much of southern Africa (Zimbabwe and South Africa, to name just two countries) doing readings. It was a true "Babylon by bus" experience, including being held up at Harare Airport because one of the poet's Djembe drums didn't have a serial number—kai!

After dinner, a monkey, and a mint or two, Dawes and I got to sharing ideas about projects. We talked about the African Poetry Book Fund as well as a folio series of emerging poets' work. The box set is the end result of that conversation. Everything I have laid out shows the fragmented but truly cosmopolitan identity and journey of Africanness toward a self that holds multiple identities, something the African literary critic at Princeton University, Wendy Belcher, calls "a wardrobe of selves."

To argue, at this point, who is or is not African, and how to categorize that, is to go back to 1964, to that famous conference in Makerere, where men and women tried in vain to answer the same. The source is not as important to us here as where it goes and into what it blossoms. Or as my grandfather once said, the discoverer, Mungo Park, was a fool to seek the source of the Niger. "We know it comes from somewhere near," he said, but more significantly, "Where does it go? What does it become?"

What unites these poets is the compulsion to articulate the postmodernist mentality that has recently marked the African consciousness, to attempt a continental and global self that is expansive enough to flow like the Niger but never loses the nation that birthed it. And there is more. The most significant things hip-hop achieved were making the world a smaller place, creating a lifestyle, a music, and an entire worldview that remains ever renewing, ever youthful. TJ Dema, a spoken-word poet of tremendous skill and a founder of spoken word in Botswana, struggles, as Matthew Shenoda so eloquently states in his introduction to her book, to merge an ancient African orality with a global youth culture often performed and not codified in written form, to find a language and craft that arrests the rapidly improvised and changing world of spoken word just long enough for us to read it—before it wheels and comes again.

This journey to language—to a codification of nation and self and globalization—to create a craft so different from that pulled by the generations before, marks every poet in this collection. The vastness of this negotiation of selves works itself out in Clifton Gachagua's work in a new strain of cosmopolitanism and a tone reminiscent of the American Lyric form but laced with a dangerous subversive wit and turn, not just of phrase, but of worldview. Breathtaking. Tsitsi Jaji is as Zimbabwean as her name, and yet she breaks free of the shackles of expectation of the obvious liberation song expected of African poetry to play in a new equally subversive medium. Jaji's words are subtly transformative, providing a seedbed into which these ideas mature and flower. Hers is an Africa rarely seen in the West, one that colonizes rather than is colonized.

In the poetry of Nick Makoha from Uganda, we settle into the complex alchemy of turning trauma into the material of life, of transubstantiation. Yet as much as this work is based on the devastating narrative of postcolonial Africa, the power of Makoha's poetry, the place where his voice joins that of Walcott and, perhaps, even Yeats, is in the elevation of ordinary lives into metaphors of poetic redemption. Even that one ordinary life lived outside the matrix of traumatic politics, by the very need to live, is enough to hang so much on. Ladan Osman's power, as Ted Kooser wisely says, is to put her hand squarely on the reader's heart. She does this with an awe that is so unaffected, so ordinary, that we are left shaken and believing in the project of redemption experienced in Makoha's writing. Osman's work leads the reader, deceptively by questioning, to new places of realization. But it is an inquisitiveness that is almost relentless and so unadorned as to demand engagement, an answer, or an admission of one's inability to do so. With a simple turn of phrase, she brings the heart back without guile.

The work of the Somali poet, Warsan Shire, left me devastated, uplifted, and, quite simply, in awe. Despite her extreme youth, she echoes Yvonne Vera of Zimbabwe who weaves an unflinching and original song in books such as *Butterfly Burning*.

Len Verwey continues this negotiation in a chapbook of remarkable balance, with poems that put their fingers right into the wounds of the continent and emerge with a handful of light. These poems challenge everything we expect from an African poet. Verwey writes about heartbreak and love, yet maps war, loss, and dance in a language that holds all without contradiction. These gifted poets carry our history and our future with an easy grace. For this, I thank them.

Recently, I found out that the word Yoruba, the name for one of the mightiest, most brilliant, and enduring African nations, was coined by the neighboring country of the Nupe. The word simply means "those people." This is what it means to be African—to name "those people," a people made up of no less than eleven small nation states, a people whose religion is as old and complex as Hinduism and still flourishes in the wake of four hundred years of Western Christian influence. These are people of one word that holds both awe and dismissal, which allows multiple identities and even cosmologies to coexist, and yet affirms each one; this is what the APBF collection of chapbooks has achieved. We offer you "these people"—Kenyan, Botswanan, Zimbabwean, Ugandan, Somali, Mozambique—poets, Africans, nomads.

Enjoy.

—Chris Abani
Los Angeles/Chicago

The Chapbooks of
Seven New-Generation African Poets

Carnaval by Tsitsi Jaji
with a preface by Nii Ayikwei Parkes

The Cartographer of Water by Clifton Gachagua
with a preface by Chris Abani

Mandible by TJ Dema
with a preface by Matthew Shenoda

Ordinary Heaven by Ladan Osman
with a preface by Ted Kooser

Otherwise Everything Goes On by Len Verwey
with a preface by Gabeba Baderoon

Our Men Do Not Belong to Us by Warsan Shire
with a preface by Bernardine Evaristo

The Second Republic by Nick Makoha
with a preface by Kwame Dawes

INTRODUCTION TO
EIGHT NEW-GENERATION AFRICAN POETS: A CHAPBOOK BOX SET
2015

Featured poets: Peter Akinlabi, Viola Allo, Inua Ellams, Liyou Libsekal, Amy M. Lukau, Vuyelwa Maluleke, Blessing Musariri, Janet Kofi-Tsekpo

Featured artist: Imo Nse Imeh

Introduction in Two Movements

Part One

The plan is simple, as publishing plans go. Publish seven to ten chapbooks by African poets each year. Promote said chapbooks. In ten years there will be seventy to one hundred chapbooks by African poets that might not have existed before. Oh, and make sure the work is first-rate, representative, and new. This plan only works if there are seven to ten really gifted African poets who have not yet had a major publication. This only works if you know how to find them. This only works if you have a team of brilliant editors willing to help select and, where necessary, nurture these poets. This only works if you have the resources to do it. With the inimitable and generous Chris Abani as coeditor, and with a supportive team of editors—Bernardine Evaristo, Gabeba Baderoon, John Keene, and Matthew Shenoda—to assist in the selection and introduction writing, we had the team that could make this happen. Finally, with a great bequest by Laura Sillerman, the project had the funding support needed to make it all possible.

In our first year we collaborated with Slapering Hol Press to produce an exciting box set, *Seven New-Generation African Poets*, with a roster of poets who were already positioned to embark on impressive publishing careers.

Of the seven poets included, four are currently anticipating publication of their debut full-length books. The other three will see first collections in the next two years. We dare not take credit for these successes; that was never the point. What we take some joy in is the fact that the series has generated the kind of interest in African poetry that we have not seen in a long time. This is a good thing. Any anxiety that there is not ample talent to sustain such a project has proven to be absurd.

This year, Akashic Books has assumed the role of publisher and has brought its remarkable savvy and creative brilliance to the project. This year's lineup of poets has grown to eight, and the quality of the poetry remains as stellar as ever. *Eight New-Generation African Poets* features poets from the Cameroon, Nigeria, Ghana, Ethiopia, South Africa, Zimbabwe, and Angola, as well as the US and the UK where some of these poets now reside. The poems open up spaces of the African imagination that are varied in their topical interests, but consistently alive with surprise and energy. Several of these poets reflect the more recent African diaspora, and so they offer us a complex of identities that are negotiated though the demands of the poetic project of using language to somehow express their sense of the world.

For some people who follow African poetry, who have attended readings by poets in clubs and halls in Harare or Cape Town or London, these names will not be unfamiliar. For people paying close attention to literary journals and online poetry sites around the world, these names may ring a bell. The point is that these are poets whose work reflects a striking clarity of voice and aesthetics that speaks to their long experience at the craft in some instances, and to their uniquely refreshing genius in others. At the end of the day, the chapbooks are a delight to read and continue to reinforce what we have been certain about since this project began, that African poetry is rich with variety and poetic complexity. Of course we went out in search of the poets. And we got important help along the way.

Many of the poets we considered were introduced to us by people like the writer and literary activist Beverley Nambozo of Uganda. Others came from writers in the UK and the US, and still others came to our attention in contests like the Sillerman First Book Prize and the Brunel University African Poetry Prize. We scoured venues like the Badilisha Poetry podcast site to find voices that might engage us. We read manuscript after manuscript to narrow things down to these eight.

We can conclude that African poetry is varied, vibrant, earnest, and brimming with the energy and intelligence we enjoy in the best poetry. But each of these writers demonstrates something else—a distinctive voice that is fresh and compelling. These are urgent voices as engaged with the politics of human existence as with the beauties of the world we live in. If you read these chapbooks, I am confident that you will not quickly forget these names: Liyou Libsekal (Ethiopia), Vuyelwa Maluleke (South Africa), Amy M. Lukau (US/Angola), Inua Ellams (Nigeria/UK), Viola Allo (Cameroon/US), Peter Akinlabi (Niegria), Blessing

Musariri (Zimbabwe), and Janet Kofi-Tsekpo (UK/Ghana). The art gracing the covers of these chapbooks comes from the remarkable Nigerian artist Imo Imeh.

Our hope, though, is that we are not simply introducing these poets to a Western readership, but indeed, first and foremost, to an African readership. One of the sad ironies of the situation with poetry in Africa is how infrequently published work crosses the borders of the various nation-states and regions of the continent. Some of the writers are part of a growing circuit of spoken-word poetry in larger cities, and for those able to attend festivals there is a chance to hear some of these poets. But given the challenges of publishing and distribution on the continent, the books are not making that journey, and while one can overvalue the importance of the published work, one must never underestimate its value as a critical source of artistic and cultural memory for our societies. This box set, we hope, will do that work in meaningful ways.

—*Kwame Dawes*

Part Two

I am often nostalgic and like to return to origin stories. About how this set of books, this publishing intervention, was fleshed out during the Poetry Africa tour we were part of. While in Zimbabwe, we encountered the most beautiful moments—being able to touch Paleolithic rock paintings made by our ancestors so long ago it beggars the imagination—and a generosity amongst poets and writers that we could all use. And also an anger, a justified one. Zimbabwe (like many African countries, including my own) is a difficult place to live, much less to make art—the result of misguided leaders. Africans are engaged politically and humanely with the need to find languages and modes of confrontation with this overwhelming difficulty. But that anger often lacks the shape and the language or even aesthetic framework that it needs.

This became sadly evident when Kwame Dawes was about to give a talk at the Book Café in Harare on Bob Marley—as poet, as musician, as political activist, as artist—and the house deejay was playing bad club music. Kwame asked repeatedly for the music to be changed to Bob's discography. Bob was a sellout, the young deejay said glibly. Kwame delivered a stern talking-to about the misguided ideas the young man had, about the inability to see a craft that was truly African, an aesthetic response that had been thought through rather than delivered blithely, angrily even, as a sound bite. Chastened, the deejay let Bob's "No Woman, No Cry" fill the room, the very song that Nobel Prize–winning poet Derek Walcott had said was a poem he wished he could have written—that very moment a revelation in itself, of hope and the transformation of our own selves by our own minds.

It bears saying that everything in African poetry and even music reminds one of the way reggae music, in its three and a half beats over four per bar count, dips into the "chekem," as Kwame Dawes explains in his book *Natural Mysticism: Towards a Reggae Aesthetic*. That lyric dip contains all the ineffable expression of the middle passage, its attendant melancholy, and the condition of trying to shape a new national identity for Jamaica, and yet it retains all the glorious transformative history of Africa. The turn that transforms reggae songs into poems of endless yearning that oddly satisfies us, where the yearning is the arrival and not the satiation. A turn that allows a simultaneity of expression, sometimes contradictory, to exist, making a reggae song part praise, part sorrow and lament, part political chant, part love song, and much more.

This is the turn we find in this new African poetic moment. A poetics that struggles to connect the global sweep of Africans with their ancestral past, with their possible future, all Achebe, all Ifa chant, all hip-hop, and all simultaneous: a simultaneity embodied in that moment in which I stood next to Lebo Mashile, in front of an ancient Neolithic rock painting of an elephant, reaching across a small trench to touch it, while listening to Bob Marley's "Trenchtown Rock" on my iPod, while the guide who brought us was wearing a FUBU tracksuit with dress shoes—a true "chekem" if there ever was one. This is a turn in reggae that has its roots in Africa and that made reggae the formative musical form of modern African political identity, from Egypt to the Cape. So always we are confronted with new ways to think about being African, to think about that term at all and not limit ourselves to definitive ethnic nationalities, but rather to spread wider. In these new poets, clear, strong, and prominent voices, we begin to see the negotiation of a kind of modernist thought on the continent that the early rush to nationalism and to nationalize nascent states interrupted. It is always reassuring to me to see this being struggled with by the continent's writers, who I have often called the curators of our humanity.

Here in these chapbooks, in the lyrical composition of the poets, I welcome you to a new African lyric dip. At once lament, at once protest, at once love song, at once incantation of hope and a clear future, at once entertaining, at once a new direction and a link in a chain of a human African achievement, an unending lineage of light.

—*Chris Abani*

The Chapbooks of
Eight New-Generation African Poets: A Chapbook Box Set

Bearing Heavy Things by Liyou Libsekal
with a preface by Gabeba Baderoon

Bird from Africa by Viola Allo
with a preface by Chris Abani

Mitu's Spice Tour by Blessing Musariri
with a preface by Bernardine Evaristo

A Pagan Place by Peter Akinlabi
with a preface by Matthew Shenoda

Things We Lost in the Fire by Vuyelwa Maluleke
with a preface by John Keene

Who Are You Looking For? by Amy M. Lukau
with a preface by Karen McCarthy Woolf

The Wire-Headed Heathen by Inua Ellams
with a preface by Matthew Shenoda

Yellow Iris by Janet Kofi-Tsekpo
with a preface by Chris Abani

INTRODUCTION TO
TATU: NEW-GENERATION AFRICAN POETS, A CHAPBOOK BOX SET
2016

Featured poets: D.M. Aderibigbe, Gbenga Adesina, Kayombo Chingonyi, Safia Elhillo, Chielozona Eze, Nyachiro Lydia Kasese, Ngwatilo Mawiyoo, Hope Wabuke

Featured artist: Victor Ehikhamenor

Part One
But Who Is Counting? We Are.

It is impossible to introduce the third box set of chapbooks by African poets without reflecting at least briefly on what has transpired since we embarked on this splendid adventure. In short, good and exciting things have been happening. African poets are being published and their work is encouraging us to think about aesthetics, poetics, and the business of publishing in useful and necessary ways.

Since each chapbook in this box set has been introduced with insight and generosity by a cluster of remarkable poets, our reflections here will not assume the traditional role of looking in close detail at the work you will find in the collection, but instead, we reflect, albeit tentatively, on the position of poetics in

African writing today. These collections are demanding from us exactly this kind of discussion, so we hope that these thoughts will trigger even more discussions around this subject in the future.

To date, Warsan Shire, Clifton Gachagua, Ladan Osman, Nick Makoha, and Len Verwey, all poets from our first box set, have secured contracts for full-length volumes or have already seen released their first full-length books of poetry. The African Poetry Book Series will release four new titles in 2016 featuring poetry we have solicited or have received over the transom by some remarkable African writers, as well as a new volume of our "New and Selected" series from a major African poet, Gabriel Okara. Our third Sillerman First Book Prize winner, Mahtem Shiferraw's collection *Fuchsia*, will also appear in 2016. We are, understandably, I think, quite excited about these developments, and that excitement increased this year when we started to receive the manuscripts of poets recommended to us from contacts around the world, and poets we had encountered in the various prizes we have judged that feature African poets for this box set.

I was recently at the Berlin International Poetry Festival, which, along with its counterparts in Rotterdam and Medellin, happens to be a regular meeting place for poetry festival directors from all over the world. The ambitious and hustling "world poet" does well to be at these events in what can often feel like a setting for auditions, networking "encounters" in the style of a poetry job fair since these directors are, one senses, constantly in search of new talent for their events. It is, of course, a good thing. But it is also an occasion for these directors, punters, and scouts to talk about the challenges they face. So many people came to me first to thank the African Poetry Book Fund for allowing them at least one central place where they can find a number of African poets; and secondly for the fact that these box sets and the books we have been publishing have allowed them to seek out the African poets through a mechanism other than the usual web crawl through YouTube and Vimeo for examples of the performances of these poets.

I have a complex of feelings about this development since, on one hand, I value greatly the rich tradition of performance that thrives in African poetry today; and on the other, I do worry that more often than not, publishers, programmers, and other players in the poetry world have felt comfortable with the circumstance that relegates African poetry to performance only. They do so sometimes for noble reasons, like respecting the importance of the oral tradition and the explicitly stated views by many African poets that their work is written primarily for performance. However, the *effect* of this position is hardly noble, nor is it, in fact, a product of genuine examination.

A quiet debate taking place among African poets surrounds the "authenticity" of this notion of performance as it pertains to the wave of spoken word performance that dominates much of what one could ambitiously call the poetry stages in many African countries today. Several African poets have made it clear that their emergence as writers, their empowerment as performers and poets, owes a great deal, if not everything, to the explosion of spoken word performance that emerged in the US in the late 1980s and 1990s with an explicit rootedness in the hip-hop aesthetic and culture. Many more do not say this explicitly, but it is clear from their work that this is the dominant influence on their ideas of what is valid poetry. The conscious performers of that generation were fully aware that spoken word poetry predated the emergence of hip-hop, but all would agree that hip-hop was the core aesthetic of the spoken word movement which, like hip-hop, spread its tentacles all over the world.

And this is not to undervalue the role of great artists like Linton Kwesi Johnson and Gil Scott Heron and the hundreds of artists who mastered the art of performance. The power of hip-hop has been its capacity to be adopted and adapted to various cultures around the world, and the countries of Africa have been no exception. However, it is important to recognize that the spread of hip-hop is inextricably tied to the spread of American capitalism and broader corporate imperialism, and to recognize it as another of the many inevitable sociopolitical forces that have come to shape most modern societies even as they have either embraced, mimicked, resisted, or reinterpreted those forces to suit their own realities and their traditions.

That last sentence, of course, should be tempered by a recognition of another important fact, which is that the spread of hip-hop and its attraction to African writers as well as writers of color around the world is part of a larger and positive Pan-Africanist movement that celebrates (and has for centuries) the ways in which Africans from around the world are finding common ground and connection through shared ideas of art and culture. If we do away with the notions of "purity," we may be able to celebrate the persistence of solidarity between people of African descent despite systematic efforts to break that connection. However, I point to the fluidity of cultural influence and change because it demands of us a willingness to recognize that Africa's heterogeneity of history and culture is elemental to the art that is created there.

In other words, the efforts to presume that the "Africanness" of "African Poetry" is defined by performance, while "African Poetry" that is written and published amounts to an imperial colonizer's imposition, is reductionist, limiting, and insulting, as it underestimates the extent to which, in dynamic and evolving cultures, the artists are willing to engage a range of possibilities to advance art and its relevance to their times and to their societies. Culture is flux, flux is culture.

Above all, what we hope for is a poetics that is more African than it has ever been, but we are in the business of trusting the African poet to discover what this Africanness means. It may well emerge as something quite specific, something located with a particular tribe, ethnic group, neighborhood, or community, or it may grow out of some visionary insight into the ways in which Africa as a continent is changing.

The African Poetry Book Fund is a project, then, that seeks to undermine the easy ways of reducing Africa to notions that do not recognize the complexity and variety of experiences and practices that constitute poetry written by Africans. In many ways, it would be tempting to try to offer some definitive statement about what African poetry is, but this would be a silly thing to attempt, and, at the end of the day, such exercises belong to our colleagues in academia and not to us in our capacity as editors. It strikes me as more critical to at least make us see what African poets at home and abroad are writing. All of these poets share one thing in common: they consider themselves Africans and do so not as individuals of the historical diaspora, which created new nations of people of African descent in the Americas and in parts of Europe, but as individuals who have an immediate and very recent connection to Africa, either as residents or as what we like to call immigrants. It is important that they consider themselves Africans both for academic reasons and for practical reasons: the project is called the African Poetry Book Fund, after all.

Yet even as I am unwilling to offer a prescription of what makes an African poem African, I certainly am enthusiastic about observing that African poets are writing poetry of great variety, range, and complexity in terms of styles, forms, and subject matter. I am enthusiastic about the ways in which the varied backgrounds, language groups, cultures, and histories that make up this diverse continent are all reflected in the poetry that these poets are producing.

But I do not want to pretend that the editing of this box set and this series has not been a product of the distinctive tastes of Chris Abani and myself. By this, I mean there is nothing unusual about this series, as series go. Editors have their biases and inclinations, and these are reflected in the selections they make. They are also reflected in the ways we have edited the collection. But we are also teachers, editors of long standing, and serious readers of poetry from all around the world and within the long tradition of African poetry. Thus, we come with a broader sense than most of what might prove interesting and effective in poetry. We are also as interested in taking the aesthetic inclinations of the poets seriously and challenging them to bring to these goals a full command of craft. We believe that the more options an artist has, the greater the choices he or she will make. And so we are proud of the eclectic nature of the work in this box set. There is no prescriptive content at work here, but instead, above all, we find the work urgent, well-crafted, and beautifully and movingly evocative.

Perhaps it was subconscious doubt that led us to name the first box set in a manner that did not suggest a series that would go on to be published each year for at least ten years as we initially conceived of it. We simply called it *Seven New-Generation African Poets*. Since the second was distinguished by the increased number of poets featured, we kept up this pattern of ignoring the fact that at some point we would need to find other ways to distinguish one volume from the next, and called it

Eight New-Generation African Poets. Due to the fact that we had managed to come to an agreement with Akashic Books to publish with them three iterations of the box set before reviewing the relationship, and the more practical fact that this third box set contains eight featured poets, we were prompted by Johnny Temple of Akashic Books to tackle the issue once and for all. By tagging on to our new title the word *tatu*, a Swahili word denoting the number three, we are codifying our faith and confidence that this is truly a series—and our ambition to ensure that it continues to exist in the world.

—*Kwame Dawes*

Part Two
Contending with the Ghosts

In the tradition of written poetry in Africa, in recent times, and within the Anglophone tradition, Christopher Okigbo stands tall. Very few continental poets, in any language, have approached his power (with the exception perhaps being Kofi Awonoor and Dennis Brutus), in terms of the prophetic, the singularity of voice, and the ability to meld so effectively the Western forms of his education with those of the traditional forms he came out of—proverbs, song, chant, and incantation. In this, perhaps, he surpasses all others of his generation and even generations to come. In his poem "Come Thunder" (and the slim volume of poems titled after it), we see the full effects of Yeats, of the Romantics, but also of the funerary chant of the Igbo, the invocatory chanting of traditional priests and something else, something entirely Okigbo.

I bring this up not to pit the written text against the oral, or to suggest that the only way forward is the merging of Western and African poetic aesthetics (even though we have seen Wole Soyinka do it effortlessly in drama), but rather to say that intertextuality can only enrich what is already rich tradition. I also want to draw attention to the efficacy of the written form, in terms of distribution and endurance and therefore influence.

Part of our decision to publish as many emerging poets as we can comes from this desire to ensure that there is a body of work available to generations to come.

While it would be naïve and perhaps untrue for me to pretend that positioning African poetry in the Western imagination in new ways is not important, what is more important for us is creating a conversation among the poets working continentally and across the diaspora, not just about what is or what isn't African poetry, but to open up aesthetic expressions not previously encountered.

It is already a limited project in spite of the fact that (with this collection included) we have published twenty-four new poets (and, as Kwame Dawes notes, some of whom have gone on to publish first books and create careers), because to truly be as Pan-African as Kwame and I see it, we would need to be able to translate work from the many languages that written work is produced in on the continent, from Hausa to Shona, and also from the main languages of colonial conquest, like Arabic, French, and Portuguese. Yet we must begin somewhere and hope that this momentum will help our goals expand and grow.

Many of the African freedom and anticolonial movements had their formations in the slave revolts of Jamaica and Haiti, and later the civil rights movements of the United States. Some of what it means to be a modern African has been shaped by conversations started in the diaspora, and so it seems only fitting that the aesthetic conversation within African poetry include those voices in the dialogue.

African fiction has already broken through this in ways that leave us all with no doubt that African novelists rank amongst the best in the world, from Mozambique's Mia Cutto to Nigeria's Ngozi Chimamanda Adichie. For obvious reasons, like the economies of scale involved, African poetry has received no such investment and therefore lags behind the African novel in global recognition.

That African poetry still has a strong link at least in the academic sense to the oral, is not to say that orality is holding it back. Or that orality doesn't have clear structural and formal elements like those found in the written. This is not really about that kind of conversation. One only has to look at the body of oral poetry that comprises the Yoruba Ifa religious corpus, including Ijala and Iyere, among others, to see that there are clear forms and rhyme schemes, slant rhymes, punning, and the lean into the ineffable. The only difference between oral forms and written forms is the nature and range of improvisation that the oral allows.

The problem with the poem in Africa staying rooted in the oral is more political in ways that can defeat aesthetic growth. But that impulse is a ghost left over by the Negritude movement, which, all of its successes notwithstanding, created a false impression of African literature and art forms as expressions of the soul that stand against and in opposition to Western forms of the mind. This is of course not true, and yet it has persisted such that the opportunities for growth in dialogue with literatures from all over the world have been squandered.

Where hip-hop and attendant spoken word traditions tend to emphasize the performativity (as already detailed by Kwame), another form that had early influences on African artists is reggae. Where hip-hop grew out of the streets and lends itself to more improvisation and plasticity in the application across culture and country, reggae was a highly rehearsed and studio-produced form that, while embraced by musicians like Lucky Dube and Majek Fashek and bent toward the indigenous, has seen little borrowed from it other than in the political sense.

And so here we are again, eight more chapbooks and poets in, with aesthetics and politics of such differing range that they strain to come together cohesively in one collection—but they do; no doubt about it. New forms, linguistic play, and formal approaches proliferate. These books represent a strong emerging conversation, one that seems to be able to balance the text and the performative and remain fresh and new.

Kwame and I believe that by the time we reach perhaps the fiftieth chapbook, we will be able to finally track the trends and developments and new possibilities and even a future for African poetry. For now, it is humbling and personally enriching to be able to curate this series with Kwame Dawes.

—Chris Abani

The Chapbooks of
Tatu: New-Generation African Poets, A Chapbook Box Set

Asmarani by Safia Elhillo
with a preface by Karen McCarthy Woolf

The Color of James Brown's Scream by Kayombo Chingonyi
with a preface by Kwame Dawes

Dagoretti Corner by Ngwatilo Mawiyoo
with a preface by Yona Harvey

In Praise of Our Absent Father by D.M. Aderibigbe
with a preface by Tsitsi Jaji

The Leaving by Hope Wabuke
with a preface by Patricia Jabbeh Wesley

Painter of Water by Gbenga Adesina
with a preface by Ladan Osman

Paper Dolls by Nyachiro Lydia Kasese
with a preface by Gregory Pardlo

Survival Kit by Chielozona Eze
with a preface by Chris Abani

INTRODUCTION TO
NNE: NEW-GENERATION AFRICAN POETS, A CHAPBOOK BOX SET
2017

Featured poets: Yasmin Belkhyr, Victoria Adukwei Bulley, Mary-Alice Daniel, Chekwube O. Danladi, Lena Bezawork Grönlund, Ashley Makue, Momtaza Mehri, Famia Nkansa, Ejiọfọr Ugwu, Chimwemwe Undi

Featured artist: Ficre Ghebreyesus

Introduction in Two Movements

Part One
The Body As an Alien and Dangerous Entity

Perhaps the first thing that anyone will see when considering this box set will be the artwork that graces all the covers of these chapbooks and the box itself. The work is that of a remarkable Eritrean artist, the late Ficre Ghebreyesus, whose art we have been able to secure through the generosity and solidarity of his wife Elizabeth Alexander and his family. The compelling fascination with the body, the African body, that marks his art, seems to rhyme perfectly with the poetry that is collected here. Our project is enhanced tremendously by having the work of such an important and accomplished artist. In the end, the art lives on in beautiful and meaningful ways, through the conversations that it has with the work of other artists.

We invited about thirty-five poets to submit manuscripts for this year's chapbook box set. This is an annual ritual that we are committed to carrying until we arrive at the tenth year of publishing the chapbooks of a new generation of African poets. Each year, the task gets more and more difficult. The quality of the manuscripts is extremely impressive. The range of the work we are getting is equally striking, representing poets living in Africa and those of African heritage living in the recent African diaspora. More and more people are sending us the names of poets who they believe would do well to be considered for the series, and so making the selection has become a greater and greater challenge for Chris Abani and myself—but it is a challenge that we welcome. It confirms a hunch we have had for a while that given the possibility of a thoughtful, well-edited publishing entity for their work, the African poets will emerge. We are not *discovering* poets. This should be clear from any brief look at the poets we are publishing here. All of them are serious writers who have been engaged with the world of publishing, having had individual poems published in literary journals and anthologies around the world, and having won fellowships, awards, and prizes for their writing. For many who follow the writing of poets of color or who pay attention to the spoken word scene, some of the names listed here will not be strange at all. A few are at the final stages of putting together their debut collection of poems, and others can be read online. Yet, for many of them, their presence in this singular gathering of African poets is an important step, and there is something extremely exciting about seeing the ways in which they have engaged this complex idea of Africanness with their work.

There are some striking features of this year's box set. Firstly, despite our efforts to keep the number of chapbooks collected here to seven or eight, we were unable to reduce the number to less than ten. Indeed, a few of the collections that are not included may well have been included had we the resources to do so. Secondly, it will be clear that of the ten poets collected here, nine of them are women. On the surface this seems remarkable, but while we have not tried to understand why this is the case, we welcome it as an exciting development in African poetry, which has, for many decades, been wholly dominated by male voices. Finally, a significant proportion of the selections here represent poets who either currently live outside of Africa or spend their time moving back and forth between Africa and the rest of the world. The African Poetry Book Fund has been working hard to maintain a pair of core principles in the work that we do that may seem contradictory, but in practice prove to be necessary ways of approaching the work that we do. On one hand, we have sought to give as much attention to finding and supporting the work of poets who are living and working in African countries where many of the opportunities for publication and formal mentorship are limited. To this end, we have developed a fairly exciting network of partners all across the continent and this has proven to be an exciting development for us. At the same time, we have sought to recognize that so many of the poets from Africa have found homes outside of the continent for reasons that may have little to do with their poetry careers, but have more to do with the complex circumstances of life that have led to our people being a people of migration and transcultural movement. And we have held to the view that many of these poets living outside of Africa have had an equally difficult time finding communities that share their own experience and may even understand their distinctive aesthetics and concerns as poets. By tackling these two goals at the same time, we have been enacting the larger principles of Pan-Africanism with the caution of not attempting to totalize the experience of African people.

But here is the truth: notwithstanding these necessary considerations of geography, culture, and gender, what we have been thrilled by is the quality of the poetry that is collected here. There is a startling intelligence running through each of these collections, but beyond it all, I have left this process of working closely with manuscript after manuscript with a sense that the singular thing that connects these books is the way in which these poets root the emotional and intellectual explorations in the body—the body as an alien and dangerous entity that is negotiating its presence in a world that is sometimes hostile, sometimes welcoming, but always forcing the poet to resist erasure and invisibility.

I decided to create a collage of these instances in the collection that continue to remind me of the varied concerns of these poets and, at the same time, the collective.

In Lena Bezawork Grönlund's *Everything Here*, she describes the legacy of the bodies of her parents on her body in an alien Swedish landscape: "I look at him / with her thin shoulders / against the wall, his thin face, / his startled look, and her deep lines / under my eyes." ("Still Life")

In Famia Nkansa's collection *Sabbatical*, she explores the theme of visibility and invisibility: "do you see this me, more than I could even be, or the me that me and everyone else would see if we only took the energy to look hard enough?" ("it is from my need to matter than I ask you this")

In her poem "mom's on fire," in her collection *i know how to fix myself*, Ashley Makue observes, "my mother is a war zone

/ they don't tell her that / these men that pee in her / and leave with gunpowder in their chests."

Victoria Adukwei Bulley's collection, *Girl B*, is filled with exquisite transgressions of the body like this: "Hair coming down past your breasts like confetti. Your straighter teeth, your stripped upper lip (recoiling still), your clean, dark complexion. Lean thighs, or the gap between them. The grasp of your jeans at you like a lover that you'd like to leave, exposing the gap." ("Girl")

And here, in Chimwemwe Undi's poem "On Sickness" (*The Habitual Be*), she invokes Lucille Clifton's defiance of various enemies of the black woman's body: "The dark perfection of this body / is disallowed from cracking. / Won't you celebrate with me, / nonwhite & woman, how / I can but may not name / the thing I know is / trying to kill me."

In Yasmin Belkhyr's provocative exploration of religion and piety in her poem "Eid Al-Adha," she engages notions of the body and the violence it is capable of. She writes: "There are so many bodies of mine that I haven't claimed yet. So many versions, so many lives. Fat purple figs and all that. When I speak of bodies, I mean: I'm afraid of mine. When I speak of bodies, I mean: I wonder what yours is capable of. When I speak of bodies, I mean: there is too much inside of me . . ." (*Bone Light*)

Mary-Alice Daniel contemplates what we end up doing with the body in science and in the world of exhibitions, which calls to mind what was done to Ota Benga at the turn of the last century: "You can do to a body a lot of things. / A feature in *Smithsonian* on cannibals makes me hungry. // I'm learning so much—they use bodies as ritual snacks, / eating everything but teeth, hair, and penis." ("Blood for the Blood God")

For Chekwube O. Danladi, the body's capacity for pleasure and the exploration of profound sensuality is directly connected to its capacity to be broken, its unsettling vulnerability. In "Communion" she writes: "No one has a body that cannot be broken. / I shatter beneath a windowsill, separate as fruit / for provender: pomelo breasts, / lemondrop melon ass, a head / of ripened cantaloupe." (*Take Me Back*)

In the elusively elliptical prose poems in her chapbook *sugah. lump. prayer*, Momtaza Mehri occasionally anchors the reader in a meditation on a subject that is full of sensual and psychic complexity, as in her poem about the body, "In that order." Again, vulnerability is tempered by agency and desire: "my body gives way to salt gives way to a bruised telephone line gives way to honeyed mahalibya tones gives way to the corner of your mouth gives way to I can smell it on you gives way to that russet-mustached soldier on the cheapest stamp gives way to the letters gives way to burnt sukkar gives way to caramel ripple gives way to slipping on cotton socks gives way to slippery men gives way to // dissolve."

Finally, in Ejiọfọr Ugwu's *The Book of God*, we find the poem "Magun," which beautifully renders mutation of the man's body into a vessel—a boat that must traverse various waterways. "I am a sea child. / I armpitted my paddle, / my boat on my head, / and set out for the sea under. / What is it with me and / the life of swamps?"

Each of these chapbooks has been introduced by poets of great accomplishment and insight in their own right. It is a sign of the generosity of the community that is taking shape around the African Poetry Book Fund that we have little trouble finding poets of significant standing willing to write insightful and generous introductions to each of these chapbooks. Thus it is important to thank Karen McCarthy Woolf, Ladan Osman, Honorée Fannone Jeffers, Patricia Jabbeh Wesley, Tsisi Jaji, Matthew

Shenoda, Aracelis Girmay, and Tijan M. Sallah for their work in support of these poets.

Finally, managing this complex project has been the inimitable Ashley Strosnider, whose editorial eye and brilliant administrative skill and insight have been essential to the success of this project.

—*Kwame Dawes*

Part Two
The Poem is a Body and the Body a Poem

"Every story I create, creates me. I write to create myself."
—Octavia E. Butler

The poem is a body and the body a poem. This is not something I can prove, nor even something that is necessarily true, but it does have the ring of truth about it. This is a more intuitive relationship but one I think we are all fairly conversant with and one with which most poetry lovers will agree. The one true topography of self we can chart, navigate, and map is the body. The visible self leads to the more ethereal and ineffable parts of self, the parts that poetry tries to give symbolic meaning to, to invoke that presence. And if we look closer, we see that it's not just that language gives the body presence, shape, resistance, love, affirmation, and intervention. And it is not just that the bodies of particular poets give their language a certain shape and definition, but rather that in the end, our particular idiosyncratic languages are our bodies. We exist only in the space of that language, and we use it to move a craft forward, to draw and redraw the limits of the self, both internal and external. We can argue that this is poetry's true power, to shape reality—and that is truly what power is: the choice and ability to redraw and recast our personal narratives.

No body has been more colonized, commoditized, traumatized, and dehumanized than the black body, and by definition, the African body. From the earliest ways that Europe plundered our cultures, histories, sciences, discoveries, and resources to the most recent holocaust of slavery, the legacy of these violences is still being fought the world over. So it has been particularly important to offer space and staging ground for these reclamations of the body.

From the ways that global capitalism and racism, patriarchy, and the other forms of repression have restricted and attempted to own and commodify the black body, the poems and poets represented here (and in our previous box sets) are a vanguard and growing archive of resistance and rearticulation of self. So geography, culture, and gender have become the hallmarks of these poems.

One of the things Kwame Dawes and I have struggled to maintain is the ratio of diaspora to continental poets. This is a struggle because diaspora poets do have better access to workshops and other spaces of craft education and are often better poised at the submission stage to be better poets.

As Kwame has pointed out, it is a difficult call to make because while we recognize the need for the curating we have undertaken, we are mindful of its dangers. We are mindful not to try to referee who is an African, or what constitutes or doesn't constitute Africanness. We worry that our curating will leave out voices that are vital to a more rounded African poetry archive either stylistically, aesthetically, linguistically, geographically, or in terms of gender. This is always a worry for the curator/editor; we know on the one hand that we are, intentionally or not, creating a representational archive while desperately seeking to create an all-inclusive and encompassing one. We don't want to be seen as saying *this* is African poetry, but rather, here are some of the new conversations happening in this art form, within this particular cultural moment, by these poets of African descent living on or off the continent.

You see, not only is the poem the body, or at least the simulacrum of the body, the book (or the poetry collection, which is not always a book anymore) is itself the body, maybe of the poet, but definitely of the poet's imagination. What we are beginning to see emerge, with this archive, is definitely a body. It is a body of work that is attempting to define something already and always in flux: a growing culture, a changing culture, an expanding zeitgeist, and an ever-evolving moment. This body of African poetry is exciting, and like all true simulacra, it has outgrown its original code, it has become its own consciousness. We see this body, this ineffable self in dialogue with itself—through time, with all the poets that have come before, many of whom are still being shaken off for the poet to find an original voice; but also, this new generation of poets is in dialogue with itself, the poems speaking to each other, thus these poets are reforming and repositioning the archive from within, causing it to grow and expand in interesting ways.

The process itself, of selecting these poets, can be equally frustrating and humbling. Frustrating on many levels, because we have to turn down so many with so much potential, partly because the editing we have to do to make them publication-ready is beyond our current scope (and we are trying to remedy that by developing workshops to be taken to different countries on the continent). And we have to turn down so many good poets because we can only choose ten. It is humbling because of the sheer array of talent on display by poets who are so early in their careers.

And so we are back once more to the idea of the body—the alien body of blackness at risk in the West where it sometimes settles, the familiar body of blackness at home that is also at risk from internal and external forces of homogenization. But the most important thing that we see developing is that whatever these forces are that are being brought to bear on these bodies, the poetic instinct, aesthetic, and political enactments here are working against forgetting, erasure, sentimentality, nostalgia, and anomie; instead, they are leaning into reinscription, reenactments of prosody and language, and a redrawing of the body both at stasis and in flux, an idea Homi Bhabha would certainly love.

Kwame has already sampled the poems to show the spaces of resistance, slippage, and redefinition, allowing for the individuality of concerns and yet pointing assuredly to a growing archive, a body, in dialogue. If this is where we find ourselves at this time, nearly fifty chapbooks in, then we are in a good place.

—Chris Abani

The Chapbooks of
Nne: New-Generation African Poets, A Chapbook Box Set

Blood for the Blood God by Mary-Alice Daniel
with a preface by Matthew Shenoda

Bone Light by Yasmin Belkhyr
with a preface by Ladan Osman

The Book of God by Ejiọfọr Ugwu
with a preface by Patricia Jabbeh Wesley

Everything Here by Lena Bezawork Grönlund
with a preface by Aracelis Girmay

Girl B by Victoria Adukwei Bulley
with a preface by Karen McCarthy Woolf

The Habitual Be by Chimwemwe Undi
with a preface by Tsitsi Jaji

i know how to fix myself by Ashley Makue
with a preface by Honorée Fanonne Jeffers

Sabbatical by Famia Nkansa
with a preface by Kwame Dawes

sugah. lump. prayer by Momtaza Mehri
with a preface by Tijan M. Sallah

Take Me Back by Chekwube O. Danladi
with a preface by Kwame Dawes

INTRODUCTION TO
TANO: NEW-GENERATION AFRICAN POETS, A CHAPBOOK BOX SET
2018

Featured poets: Leila Chatti, Saddiq Dzukogi, Amanda Bintu Holiday, Omotara James, Yalie Kamara, Rasaq Malik, Umniya Najaer, Kechi Nomu, Romeo Oriogun, Henk Rossouw, Alexis Teyie

Featured artist: Sokari Douglas Camp

Introduction in Two Movements

Part One
The Wonderful Limitations of What we Know

Anyone who has been following the progress of the African Poetry Book Fund's Chapbook Box Set Series might have noticed that each year the number of chapbooks included in the set has been growing. This year, we have included eleven poets in the series. While the numbers have changed, nothing has changed significantly in how we have approached the series. We have continued to seek out recommendations from many people around the world who are either poets or engaged in the business of poetry and the literary arts; we have continued to pay careful attention to the submissions we receive for the Sillerman First Book Prize for African Poetry; we have continued to work closely with the Brunel International Poetry Prize to spot promising poets who have entered that important contest; we have continued to scour the Internet and some key places like the remarkable Badilisha Poetry Exchange website; we have followed blogs, news items, tweets, and Facebook in search of noise about exciting voices; and we have come to rely on the generosity and insight of the growing list of poets we have already published—to find a long list of new poets who we approach and invite to submit work for consideration for the box set.

While not comprehensive, what we do is diligent and thorough. We do not give these poets a great deal of time to put together a chapbook manuscript. We are, alas, limited by the time demands of putting out such a collection each year. This year, almost fifty poets sent us manuscripts. We selected eleven. The quality of the work could justify even more poets. But there are constraints. At the same time, what has happened is that the quality of the work has become even more impressive and exciting, making the selection extremely challenging—and exhilarating.

Yet each year we are faced with some important questions, and we can't pretend to have answers to these questions. But before I even embark on this discussion, I have to say that undergirding the selections for these box sets is the very human fact of this editorial partnership. Chris Abani and I have always been happy to engage in discussions about aesthetics, quality, prosody, style, and much else, fully aware that we do not pretend *objectivity* in how we make these selections. We are also aware that we are shaped by the wide range of poetry we have read and listened to and studied over the years, poetry especially from all parts of Africa and from the African diaspora. What we have come to perceive as *taste* has derived from the wonderful and inevitable limitations of what we know. But we are also aware of the fact that we pay a great deal of attention to the ways in which the poets we are encountering are shaping poetic discourse wherever they are. We wait for the work to come, and then we let the work affect us, and from there, we begin to think of the choices that might be made.

So a quick review of the poets we see included here indicates a heavy Nigerian presence—five of the eleven poets are Nigerian (Kechi Nomu, Omotara James, Rasaq Malik, Romeo Oriogun, and Saddiq Dzokogi). Tellingly, of the five, four of them (excepting James, who lives in the US) currently reside in Nigeria, joining Alexis Teyie from Kenya, who also resides on the continent. Six of the poets collected here (Henk Rossuow, Leila Chatti, Amanda Bintu Holiday, Umniya Najaer, Yalie Kamara, and Omotara James, as mentioned above) have *dual* places of connection if not identity, and in each case they are either US-based or living in the UK. We have been interested in the question of the extent to which residency affects or shapes the work that we get, although the APBF has always worked under the assumption that access to publishing, to books of contemporary poetry, and to a community of poets that is in dialogue with each other across nation states, will impact the quality and quantity of the poetry generated by poets based in Africa. It appears to me that the bigger question the poets are tackling is how to negotiate the multiple aesthetics of region, nation, continent, and the wider world, even as they seek to have a presence in a literary world that brings its own demands to the table. We have always sought to trust that the poets, once given the resources and encouragement to generate work with the hope of having it published or shared, will work these matters out and give us the answers based on the writing they have produced. Put another way, we have sought to have an attitude of openness and genuine interest in what these poets manage to produce and what they are passionate about whenever we have opened the doors to seeing new work and selecting it.

In a recent unpublished interview, Chris Abani made the following observation in comparing the new poets with the African poets of the past, who, he proposed, sought to find "convergences around the ideas of self":

What is surprising about this new group of poets is the aesthetic range. We've probably published more experimental poetry in the chapbook series than probably has ever been published by African poets writing in the English language. Which is remarkable. So we have everything from L=A=N=G=U=A=G=E poets, we have performance poets, we have standard lyric poets, we have narrative poets, we have poets who have found an orality in African epic forms and cast them with a modern sensibility, and so much more. We are seeing also that what may not normally be thought of as an aesthetic range is beginning to emerge. We have created an aesthetic safe space where poets themselves, whose sexuality might not be accepted within the context of their religions in Africa or their immediate culture in Africa, are using this opportunity to sort of emerge, to come out, not just in a sexual-identity way, but in ways in which that part of an African self can have a deep impact on the aesthetics that are needed to express it. So we see new forms emerge, new kinds of beauty emerge, new articulations of self emerge, and that in itself is a beautiful thing to watch.

Here, he expresses something that has been quite obvious to us, and something that has made us reluctant at this stage of matters to start making broad statements about the nature of African poetry in ways that would suggest a singular aesthetic movement or discourse. What Abani points to is that the work reflects the very eclecticism that characterizes a continent, and in this multitude of voices and sounds we find a wonderful defiance of the kind of reductionist thinking that has played no small part in excluding African poets from many important forums around the world. But Abani also goes on to affirm that we, as editors, have been beneficiaries of this richness; we have come to appreciate, through the remarkable energy and innovations of these poets, that which is possible in the emerging African poetry.

We have now arrived at our fifth box set. When this process began, the goal that made sense to us was to produce a box set each year for ten years. We are, therefore, halfway there now. The logic was to think of the number of African poets who we could see in print over a ten-year period. Already, the impact of this project confirms one basic thing that we have always suspected: the issue with African poetry has never been one of the absence of talent, but the absence of access and the lack of publishing opportunities.

—*Kwame Dawes*

Part Two
A New Conversation

And so here we are again, completing another African Poetry chapbook set, our fifth. Right off the bat, I think it is important to note that the term *chapbook* here is less about importance and more of scale; scale of production and number versus the economics of the moment that a small fund like ours has to contend with. But in terms of scope, quality, and excellence, these books are just that, books. Small though they may be, they are powerful collections of poems by poets of incredible, and still developing, talent, vision, and capacity.

In five years we have been fortunate to curate, publish, and usher into a global presence forty-four new African poets in this series. This is significant for a number of reasons—the volume of work over this short a time period has generated an intense interest in African poetry as a vibrant living force, contemporary in expression, and one that, while certainly political, has deep common human concerns at its center: love, a sense of self against tradition, technology, sexuality, and choice, to name but a few. It has also begun to generate an academic and research discussion once reserved only for African fiction.

The growing number of books over time also lets us chart, in a very concentrated way, the actual range and diversity not only of countries, gender, sexuality, and other sociological indices, but also of something else, perhaps even more important: that is the idea of an African poetics. Admittedly, as Kwame Dawes has so insightfully pointed out earlier in this introduction, we cannot pretend to have any definitive answers as to what this constitutes. But I think that this is what is most exciting about all of it. There is no longer a question about whether there is or can be an African poetics that is alive and always evolving, but rather the questions are now—are there multiple African poetics? Or multiple strands of one lineage? Or multiple lineages? Where do they converge and diverge? What are their particularities and overlaps? How are they developing? How much is that based on internal conversations? What are these conversations? What will happen to this ever-growing community of poets that are we are building? And so many more.

What we can state with absolute confidence is that this small intervention of ours (which is part of a number of interventions that the African Poetry Book Fund and its team of brilliant editors, and partners like the Brunel Prize, are achieving and implementing) has revealed rich seams of study, inquiry, aesthetic interventions, poetic pleasures, debates, and the sheer vibrancy of the often-ignored field of African poetry. A poetry that is not only uniquely African in concern, but transglobal in its expression and reach.

One of the most humanizing things I have had the privilege of doing is working with my friend, mentor, colleague, and brother Kwame Dawes on this chapbook project. I say *humanizing* because over the five or so years of doing this, I have read so much amazing poetry from African poets, continental and diasporic, and I realize every year how little anyone really knows about the capability of these poets—the ones we have come to know and the ones we haven't—and even after this enormous effort every year, how much more there is to know. The poems I have read have shown an exponential jump in engagement; they are personal, moving, and deeply engaged in the world.

From its nascent years, African literature has been inextricably linked to politics and the formation of the nation state. Prior to independence, the work of literature was often to create a sense of nation for West Africa (Fagunwa, Tutuola, Ekwensi, Achebe, Beti, Oyono, et al.) or for East Africa (Okot P'biet and Ngugi), and one can argue that all the books written by politicians like Awolowo and Azikiwe and Macaulay on their ideas for governance included the many movements like Negritude. This literature was driven by the need to create nationalist myths; to establish these new nations against their former colonial masters. While the modernist moments that helped define the nationhood of Europe, for instance, with individuals negotiating against the megalith monolith of state (even in protest, Orwell's *1984* is primarily about the individual human response to the state), African literature was engaged more directly with the nationalist agenda. I offer this not as a criticism of the time, or the writers of that moment, but as a way to suggest that nationalism was an imposing constraint on the way that literature could develop. The tone of the poets of that generation have the epic echo, the larger-than-life conflations, much like, say, Yeats was doing as Ireland fought for its independence. The new poets have been freed from this constraint by the generation or two before them. Now the poems are marked with a deep modernist sense of the self, as the locus for understanding culture, place, and politics. Gone are the tropes of ancestral drums, replaced with questions about the self.

I must point out here that neither Kwame nor myself are claiming to have much to do with this shift beyond the hard work of editorial curation and the intense work that has gone into creating and sustaining the African Poetry Book Fund (which is of course a group effort of the entire editorial board, the amazing publishing partners that we work with, and the generous donors like Laura Sillerman), but we are grateful to be the conduits, the agents of these new directions emerging into the world.

But I do offer this, and stand by these books, as evidence that there is a new conversation occurring in African poetry, amongst poets, between traditions and culture, between aesthetic movements and impulses, that is now available and accessible to poets, scholars, researchers, and students and fans of African literature, specifically African poetry, that wasn't there before this project emerged. This is a significant intervention, and has revealed to a larger world that poetry in Africa is as alive and as conversation-altering as fiction.

—*Chris Abani*

The Chapbooks of
Tano: New-Generation African Poets, A Chapbook Box Set

Acts of Crucifixion by Kechi Nomu
with a preface by Safia Elhillo

Armeika by Umniya Najaer
with a preface by Aracelis Girmay

The Art Poems by Amanda Bintu Holiday
with a preface by Kayombo Chingonyi

A Brief Biography of My Name by Yalie Kamara
with a preface by Phillippa Yaa de Villiers

Clay Plates: Broken Records of Kiswahili Proverbs
by Alexis Teyie, with a preface by Kwame Dawes

Daughter Tongue by Omotara James
with a preface by DéLana R.A. Dameron

Ebb by Leila Chatti
with a preface by Karen McCarthy Woolf

Inside the Flower Room by Saddiq Dzukogi
with a preface by Matthew Shenoda

No Home in This Land by Rasaq Malik
with a preface by Nick Makoha

The Origin of Butterflies by Romeo Oriogun
with a preface by Jericho Brown

Xamissa: The Water Archives by Henk Rossouw
with a preface by Gabeba Baderoon

INTRODUCTION TO
SITA: NEW-GENERATION AFRICAN POETS, A CHAPBOOK BOX SET
2019

Featured poets: 'Gbenga Adeoba, Hiwot Adilow, Dina El Dessouky, Ama Asantewa Diaka, Dalia Elhassan, Charity Hutete, Nour Kamel, Musawenkosi Khanyile, Daisy Odey, Salawu Olajide

Featured artist: Aïda Muluneh

Introduction in Two Movements

Part One
The Past and the Possibility of Meaning

In a lively session at the Lagos Poetry Festival in November 2018, a fascinating discussion ensued between a senior and highly regarded poet and a young, as-yet-unbooked poet. The senior poet, with sensitivity but a sense of urgency, lamented the fact that many of the younger poets were not engaged with traditions, were not engaged in the various Nigerian languages outside of English. He was rehearsing an anxiety that I have heard from senior poets around Africa, an anxiety that is sharpened by the fact that much of their own struggle as postcolonial poets and anticolonial poets was fired by a desire to create a new poetics that is not wholly dependent on Western prosody and traditions. The young woman was equally bold in her statement, and instead of railing against tradition, she simply asked, "So whose fault is that? Whose fault is it that I was raised here in Nigeria to only speak English and not to have command of any other language? Whose fault is it that I was kept away from the rituals and traditions of my culture by my family who wanted the best for me? Whose fault is it that I, as an adult, had to enroll myself into Yoruba-language classes so I could speak the language?" It was a compelling conversation about the complications of African modernity, about the sometimes widening gaps between generations of poets who have built at times quite separate notions of tradition.

These conversations can be revealing and instructive about the way that poetry is created and shaped in richly multilingual cultures where the politics of language and tradition nicely complicate the choices writers make. One Nigerian poet who grew up in the north with a father who was not from the north, said she spoke and read Hausa but had no Yoruba, her father's language, even though she now lives in the south. She negotiates her life with English. She says it is not complicated, as most people navigate language through pidgin in its varied and improvisational power. Indeed, as we read work from all over Africa, language is merely one example of the many sites for the exercising of modernity in African art and of the ways in which these writers are exploring ideas of home, of domesticity, of economics, of migration, of gender, of sexuality, without appearing to be working out of a set series of discourses. This circumstance can be unsettling to some, but it strikes me as extremely engaging and revealing in important ways.

It is no exaggeration to suggest that for many of the younger generation of African poets, the tradition that has the greatest immediate impact is the one that is associated with the spoken-word scene that has taken these countries by storm; its traditions are rooted in hip-hop and all of its attendant forces and influences. For many of these younger writers, the embrace of hip-hop was not as fraught with issues of cultural inferiority because they were being bedfellows with black people and black cultures. They have managed to skirt the complications of American imperialism that, in many ways, have come to undergird the discourse of hip-hop's world influence, but that are barely being critiqued by these artists. The great value of hip-hop, however, is the fact that there exist models within the tradition that wholly connect with the politics of resistance, of black nationalism and social progressiveness. For the poets, the slam culture and the spoken-word culture are far more defining and influential than the poetry of African poets of the twentieth century. This has created a peculiar chasm that makes the discussions between the senior poet and this young poet almost inevitable.

My comment on this matter reflects exactly what Chris Abani and I have carved out as our position with regard to what writers write about in this series. I tried to say that I am deeply interested in this debate. I am interested in the ways that the traditions of the past are being challenged and ignored and the ways that they are engaged by a sense that someone may have dropped the ball in the business of passing on a legacy of the poetic arts from one generation to the next. If, indeed, the contemporary society is wrestling between traditional culture and a new modernity, then what we desire are poets with the sensitivity, intelligence, boldness, and capacity for vulnerability to write within that moment. If, indeed, something is being lost, the poetry should enact that loss. If, as is clear, the work of the emerging poets is critiquing the past and the present as well, is engaging in hip-hop but is also fascinated by the outsider discourses of marginality that characterize much of the poetry emerging in America and the UK, especially among poets of color, then it is a good thing to see that manifest in the work. I do think that the alarm over a loss of authenticity is not unfounded, but it is misplaced. The presumption is that the authentic looks a certain way and does a certain thing.

The older poets' desire for the younger poets is fundamentally that they will be proud of their culture, that they will know that their culture has a well-developed tradition of artistry and cultural power and clarity that can rival anything, and that they should not walk around the world like orphans in search of other cultures to embrace them. But what these older poets can't be consistent about is what this confidence will look like. It would be harder for some to accept that this confidence could involve acts that are tantamount to sacrilege or acts that feel compelled to critique these traditions through the prism of contemporary society. At the same time, there is a degree of justification in being concerned that some of the younger writers, in their ambition to "break into" the literary market around the world, have decided to assume the mask of those cultures in terms of their themes, their poetics, and their discourses, and that they have sought to virtually caricature their own cultures (to affirm the view that Western societies have of the African) in an effort to secure the interest and praise of Western culture.

If the Western poetics seem fascinated by the discourse of bodies, the poets will give that world bodies. If the Western perception of Africa is that the men are patriarchal and oppressive to women and that fathers are absent, they will give them men characterized in that way. And if the view is that Africa is a place of conflict characterized by the ubiquity of child soldiers and terrorists, they will generate poems that offer this idea in spades. We are, though, not alarmed at these developments and patterns, just as we are not alarmed because so many African women are writing manuscripts with the ambition to publish, and are, consequently, being published at a rate never seen before in Africa. We are not alarmed because opportunity and exposure offer correctives that are necessary in any literary movement.

Were one to identify an echo that is remarkably consistent across the work that appears in this box set, it would summarize this discussion above in some useful ways, and it would be fraught with difficulties of discourse and ideology, because these poets are consistently positioning their parents—their fathers, even—as synecdoche of some movement toward agency and, more critically, toward an emerging poetics that is refreshingly unassured.

Ama Asantewa Diaka, in her chapbook, locates the sense of tradition within a Christian framework that permeates her work. For her the question of this faith is a place of contestation not rooted in the classic tension between West African traditional belief systems and Christianity (as a Western phenomenon), but instead as a conversation between the traditions of her parents and those of the woman who is emerging now. She thus interrogates the tenets of this faith, and she speaks of the ownership of her idea of self and belief as a departure from that of her mother. In "Let it be" she writes:

> I fret over now and tomorrow,
> giving myself and God a headache.

Spoon feed myself faith,
and come up hungry again.
I have taken up all the space on my mother's prayer sheet
and the happiness of those I love takes up all of mine.
At the end of day we're both in God's ears
saying let it be.

Legacy is complicated. But these poets are constantly engaged with the idea of heritage—fathers and mothers speak, and they are negotiating the troubles of tradition. 'Gbenga Adeoba, in "Child of the world," locates the speaker's sense of self inside the explanation of naming that comes from the father. Indeed, what we see, again and again, in these poets, is an exploration of the extent to which their destinies, as offered by parents and ancestors, are usurped by the circumstances of the present and, more critically, the emergence of "voice" as a sense of individual identity.

His father said: Son, what you seek
to drown is not a name; it is history.
His father said he was named
for the rust of songs, scars of Libya,
and the gray vaults of the sea.
He said he was named
for drowned men the world over,
his watered flax and tulips
that didn't blossom,
the dream of years withering still.

Hiwot Adilow echoes this sentiment in her work. In the title poem, "Task of the Prodigal Daughter," she places in fruitful contrast that which she was "taught to be" and that which she is. She transforms the act of prayer into an act based on touching the tangible, the felt, the "real."

> I wish I could say I am more than what I was taught to be,
> more than hurt rising to the surface to hum
> only the chord's cry, the bed left messied,
> an expanse of silence, expensive regret.
>
> I know I don't talk to God often,
> let His image straddle me instead.
> It's easier to hold the thing God made
> than admit or repent

Like Adilow, the poet Dina El Dessouky, who is of Egyptian parentage, sees her conversation with parents as transgressive, as an act of resisting old patterns and failing to meet the expectations of the parents who are represented in her poem "Food Scraps from the Dining Room":

> Mother, I am the worst kind of human.
>   I plague your house with
>   Bilharzia.
>
>   I plague your house with
>   the heresy
>   of remembering.

This complaint as characteristic of the path from tradition into the self is equally defining in another immigrant poet, this time Dalia Elhassan, who is of Sudanese heritage. She writes of her "father's absence," of the dynamics of family and relationships, but it is clear that for Elhassan, the memory of her father and her mother and her grandparents is elemental to her sense of voice and place, elemental then, to her art. In "jidu (n.): origin sudanenese," she recalls the day her grandfather died and produces yet another uncertain elegy for the "absent men":

> the day my grandfather dies I am fast asleep
> my mother wakes me up and her face is a wash of grief
>
> i wonder what I can say for all the absent men in my life
>
> i don't really remember him,
> just the wrinkle beneath his left eyebrow,
> the *'ilma* wrapped around his forehead

Here, too, is the "heresy of remembering," where remembering is transgressive because the body that remembers is acutely aware of the self—acutely aware of the separation from the past and fully engaged in the process of forging an urgent and present self.

This not only affects the poets living outside of Africa, where the distance from the past traditions seems to make obvious sense, but is also fully present in poets like Zimbabwe's Charity Hutete, who, in thinking about her father's legacy in the poem "Worse Than Wolves," finds a litany of what was not told to her as against what was told to her. She must construct her new reality out of the absence, the vacuum:

> He made no mention
> of these quasi-men who bear

> no resemblance to our fathers
> and forefathers, demigods
> who cradled us in calloused hands.
>
> Theirs is a different breed;
> a mutation with unchecked
> tongues, wayward fingers
> and unmastered man parts.

And in "The Rippers," she writes of the mother who teaches the daughter how to weave—these legacies are constantly foregrounding both the usefulness of the lessons passed on by parents and their unhelpfulness in the face of a world that is changing rapidly. Her art is about reconnecting and separation—a kind of discourse for times of change and betrayal.

Salawu Olajide, a writer based in Nigeria, recognizes that there are rich opportunities for talking about loss and remembering in the story of the West African migrants who make their way to Europe in what has now become the mythical Lampedusa narrative. His collection rehearses this terrain, and in his exploration of departure and return, we are able to see enacted the dialogue with the past and the keepers of the past, who as in other work are the parental figures—father and mother—who are generic in their character but almost always consistent in their symbolic roles. In "Kanako" the father is something of a talisman, a figure whose wisdom helps to shorten the length of the road. But even Olajide is cautious—the capacity for survival is built into the body:

> Father told me this is what happens
> when we dream. Father told me

> our bodies become birds levitating
> through the air. Father told me
> everybody carries a strange city in their body.
> Father said it is where we go when we submit
> to the heaviness of the eyes. Father told me
> Kanako only turns your road into a dream of mirage.

In this way the past and tradition are not static; instead, they amount to a lingering presence that is defined by the uniqueness of the new traveler's body: "everybody carries a strange city in their body." The mother in "After You Left" does not call for return, but she is the keeper of the guide through strange places. The flower she plants at home is meant to guide the traveler as he moves through the world:

> Your mother offers her body to the wind,
> searching for your face in towns
> where geography is learnt by the patterns on
> the palms. After you left, your mother plants a flower
> in your memory, hoping the sun
> will connect the plant and your body.

In "Naming," Nigerian-based Daisy Odey opens the collection with a poem that establishes her source, even as she speaks of her own agency in the line "I walk tongue first into myself." But she is named. She comes from somewhere. Her idea of self is troubled but shaped by the engagement with her past, represented by her father and mother:

> At birth my father named me Osun, a place. As
> I roam the world I never leave home. My mother

named me Oshun, a god. As I pray I hear my
voice call out to me to save myself.

A distant aunt says I am like my father, a well, a
thing that's always hungry. I think I am like my
mother, a wanderer.

Together these two things can only birth a river,
water that never stops running. The shore is a
woman; she doesn't taste my father in our first
kiss. Soon our clothes are on the floor, and I
think how half in itself is still whole.

South African poet Musawenkosi Khanyile's collection *The Internal Saboteur* is organized around the narrative of origin and self, and it's broken into three sections: "Father," "Mother," and "Lover"—a love interest that offers the poet a chance to construct a conception of self that is a reflection of the complex wrestling with the memory of ancestry. In this sense, memory and the cultural legacy of a family are foundational to the definition of self later on. As in most of these moments, even the past is fluid and unreliable. But this does not mean it is not necessary to contend with that memory to then address the future. A critical element of the work is how the poet seeks to acknowledge the haunting and sometimes defining presence of his parents in his decisions, and then to start to construct a narrative of separation and responsibility. It is a fit metaphor for the discovery of "voice."

Finally, we find in the poetry of Egyptian Nour Kamel, who lives and writes in Cairo, a deep consciousness from the beginning of the work that is establishing a new mythology of self that challenges patriarchal structures. In the poem "Isis in Mohandessin for my Birth," Kamel positions the goddess of the region in a kind of dialogue with the poet's own mother—it is the complex exploration of the meaning of birth that offers the occasion for the poet to consider the sense of self. Kamel's mother is important here but is an unreliable influence—the mother becomes an observer, a witness of the making of this child, and Isis is never a static figure, but one who is pushing against the norm. The movement is from the generic of belief to the quite specific of the poet's self:

> Flew through skies getting too filled forever with doomsday shade. Isis, why were you calling after me: was I stolen from the underworld by mama's will, or did you last minute bless kiss my parts together with purposeful eyes half seeing a blurred world for what it is
>
> Whatever prophecy you gave, mama said it was an omen with worrycast eyes of things to fight unarmed vulnerable because they told me I was, all mixed up too pale to be born me in the not-moon, who couldn't help wage the kind of war my legs meant me for
>
> Women's work women worry women gods! she didn't see if it was good or bad, double-glazed reflective glass, saw a lost portent of her feathered self something brief something that would kill with just a sheath, in silence looming, doubled, eat you head, first, whole.

There is something exciting about encountering in these poets not a rejection of the past, but a genuine engagement with it. And this engagement is predicated on a desire to make sense of the present. The past is fraught with contradictory impulses, and yet it offers the possibility of meaning. In many ways, these collections should be a reassuring, even if at the same time unsettling, gift for the older poets who are concerned that the contemporary poet is not engaged by the past—not engaged by the traditions of the past, if you will. What these poets demonstrate is a persistent sense that they have been shaped by their pasts, but they engage the past in the manner of the lyric self. The poetry seems engaged with ideas of the personal, but these are not memoir poems—the personal, instead, is mythologized in productive ways, allowing these writers to therefore "perform" their discourses, which thus allows for the engagement with the rich and complex and competing worlds that are pressing in on their person.

—Kwame Dawes

Part Two
The Complications of Legacy

"Legacy is complicated," to quote Kwame Dawes. Kwame says this in his anecdote about the conversation with an older poet who was complaining that the newer generations of African poets do not, in his opinion, accept or engage with the literary legacy bestowed upon them. This is at best a simple nostalgia and a refusal, knowingly or not, to engage with the true complications of legacy and literature. It is no doubt also textured with the fact that he has, in all likelihood, not read enough, if any, of the body of work he is opining about. This complication might seem obvious, but actually it is not. Even the need to articulate this comes from the experience of attempting to expand, speak to, push away from or against, and even respond to or reject the literary traditions we come from as writers and in the work we make.

The African tradition of written literature is still quite new, barely seventy years old. And when I say "written literature," I am not accounting for religious texts, colonial texts, and reports and diaries. I will account for some of this later, but I am limiting the scope to account for a more intentionally secular engagement based on a writer's desire to communicate with a reader and provide, at least, some basic artistry and entertainment. For the purposes of the work we are doing with these chapbooks to expand and continue a dialogue in literature and culture, I am considering work from the late 1940s moving forward.

This is not to disregard the wealth of indigenous writing systems that populate the continent and have done so for centuries. This includes the better-known ones like Ancient Egyptian, Ancient Meroitic, Old Nubian, Tifinagh, Osmanya, Borama, Kaddare, Mwangwego, the Nsibidi script of the Ejagham, Ibibio and Afikpo of Nigeria, and even recent ones like Mandombe, Bamum, Adlam, Bassa, Bete, Eghap, Venda, Kpelle, Loma, Mende Ki-ka-ku, N'Ko, Vai, Zaghawa, and many others. I have set aside Ge'ez and even Arabic for a different part of these notations. While many of the older forms have been linked to empire and may have been used, as in Kush, Nubia, and Egypt, to write epic poems in the service of gods and kings, they were not used in the composition and dissemination of a written literature. For the most part, literary production in Africa (and in much of the Western world) was up until recently largely the domain of the oral. This of course had to do with the low rate of literacy in written forms across the larger population. Even with the introduction of the Gutenberg press in the West, literature was still oral for the most part. It wasn't written literature that led to the survival of that technology but rather the printing of pardons for the Catholic Church. I say all this to acknowledge the arguments I know this discussion will generate, which, while quite valid, are outside the scope I am aiming for.

The truth is, with the exception of Christian and Islamic empires like those found in Ethiopia, Mali, and Songhai, the writing systems in Africa were largely the providence of male-dominated cults. So, while these orthographic systems existed all over the continent, they were used mostly in religious and occult situations as warnings to transgressors and a secret language within the cults. Some of this was to reinforce the power and fear of the cult, to divert attention from the more power-driven capitalist and (sometimes) bloodthirsty aspects of these cults, and to facilitate trade, such as the trans-Saharan and trans-Atlantic slave trades, as well.

Those parts of the continent—West, East, and North—that had fallen under the conquest of Islam and which had, in an exchange of sorts, received the gift of Arabic and its orthography, used it to produce, or acquire, store, archive, and protect what has been estimated at over a million books. In Timbuktu alone, it is estimated that somewhere near seventy thousand texts remain in existence. Some of these have deteriorated into very fragile states, having been buried sometimes for their own protection. But because of Islam's intolerance to anything not of God, most of these are Korans or interpretations or the work of science—mathematics and astronomy. Yet not very much in the way of the literature we are thinking of, at least when we refer to poets. My only qualifier here is that, since much of this work is not available to me as a reader, scholar, and writer, I can only guess at the content. This lack of access is another matter for the conversation of legacy.

Then there is the case of modern Ethiopia, known by many names over the course of history, home of the oldest Christian Church in the world, and whose religious texts were written in a language called Ge'ze. Once a widely spoken language, it has, like Latin, passed largely into obscurity and is used mostly in scriptural or scriptural-adjacent work. However, the Coptic Church and its officers didn't just write biblical work, in the strictest sense. They created a vast medieval literature that included the myths of the Queen of Sheba and many hagiographies of saints. As with all hagiography, we are confronted with part fact and part myth-making—perhaps an early form of the novel—not unlike the Gothic romances of Europe. For example, the excellently translated hagiography of the medieval female saint Walatta Petros, which contains allusions to what might be a same-sex relationship, reads almost like a novel and should be counted as a form of written literature. When we hear about medieval and renaissance African written literatures, it sounds strange even to Africans, but this is a true and real genre and phenomenon. Wendy Belcher from Princeton University has done a lot of groundbreaking work in this area, and the information is readily available. I encourage you to explore it.

You might wonder why I am writing all this. Rushing through a continental literary history in a quick snapshot? It has to do with the weight and complication of the term *legacy*, and its expressed nostalgia, fear, and an even deeper ache at its perceived loss—one that haunts many older continental writers, mostly men, interestingly enough. I am inclined to wonder though, how wide or capacious their nostalgia is. Does it include all of these contexts, all of these cultures? Does it even account for the orality that preceded the written texts? All of the endless varieties and possibilities of this vast continent, to include all the languages and all the songs? I doubt this very much. In fact, in northern Nigeria there exists, written mostly in Hausa, an immense literature produced by women writers. It is often dismissed derisively as romantic pamphlets intended to spice up the lives of women often living in harem-like conditions. Nothing could be further from the truth. These are novels, often running into several thousand pages, about love; melancholy; loss; gender imbalance; and religious, social, and domestic violence; and they express deep religious, spiritual, and mystical concerns. That these have not been translated into English or any of the other major European languages that are part of the colonial legacy of Africa, much less read, much less assimilated into what we think of as African literature, or the legacy of literature, is a loss, like so many other losses we suffer and have suffered.

It is therefore difficult to speak authoritatively of legacy when we have barely mapped the scope of said legacy. Even in this collection of chapbooks, Kwame has painstakingly tried to peel away and point to the different ways these books are attempting their engagements, and yet—and I don't think he will argue with this—he has barely touched the surface of these ten chapbooks, part of a collection of about fifty such chapbooks we have published in conjunction and conversation with first books, mid-career books, and collected full-career books. The work is vast and only just beginning. We have yet to start approaching all the many African writers whose names are not famous, arranging, scanning, and hopefully creating digital archives of their papers, a stated goal of the African Poetry Book Fund.

What this will yield in terms of legacy will take years to apprehend. Then, of course, there is the problem of translation and the lack of access to all the literatures of the continent, which both Kwame and I have discussed in other introductions. (It seems like the introductions are accounts of our humbling in the face of the work we know there is to do, and the little we have been able to do.) Even with the best of intentions, I am worried that we still think of legacy in terms of a problematic patriarchal heteronormative tradition that is held above most others. Where are the bodies of the queer in that idea of legacy? The bodies of women? Not the token few, but the fully embodied and very empowered women that exist in many oral literatures, or the many female rulers from Egypt to Ife to Kongo?

When we say legacy, what are we accounting for? The many lost languages and thus peoples? Nigeria is a country with 250 known languages, and some of these languages have as few as seven remaining speakers. What then of this vastness? How capacious is this nostalgia that we call legacy and that is often pointed as a weapon against innovation or newness? Legacy is not a static artifact; even artifacts, when broken into fragments and pieces, create new histories in an unending story of place and culture. Neither is legacy a fixed tradition. It is more like a strain of DNA that accounts for all the parts of ancestry but that holds gene sequences we are still uncovering in an ever-evolving process. This is how I think of legacy and the legacy we might be attempting to curate.

Think, if you will, in terms of technology (and language and story are primordial technologies). A legacy is a system that is still in use, many times running parallel to a newer system, which, while paving the way for the new and blending in a way to make the entire system more robust, needs updating and an overhaul. This is what I think legacy is: a verb, not a noun. A process of creating and recreating and archiving a robust system that accounts for *all* the past, as best as it can. But also is forward-looking. It is the conversation between these two processes, even when one seems to discard another, that maps the way forward.

So then, when newer writers place their imaginations in the cosmopolitan pool that is the African legacy, and expand into places that were silent before, stretching to the point of breaking a legacy, and tradition, to allow the new and the always new but once-silenced aspect of legacy to move to the center in an evolving conversation, then I believe that our legacies are safe and in good hands.

We are and always have been concerned with legacy. We are concerned with archive too, but we are not interested in the form of a classic canon decided by a few people and upheld by patriarchal systems. We are more interested in the living literature, in a living archive, in the verb of legacy. One that continues to define itself in rejection of, and in relationship to, the past, all while projecting into a possible future. The constant living dialogue between what can be, what has been, and what will be.

—Chris Abani

The Chapbooks of
Sita: New-Generation African Poets, A Chapbook Box Set

Fragments in a Closet by Daisy Odey
with a preface by Hope Wabuke

From the Zabbala's Cart by Dina El Dessouky
with a preface by Fady Joudah

Here Is Water by 'Gbenga Adeoba
with a preface by Sholeh Wolpé

In Half Light by Dalia Elhassan
with a preface by Safia Elhillo

The Internal Saboteur by Musawenkosi Khanyile
with a preface by Len Verwey

Noon by Nour Kamel
with a preface by Chris Abani

Preface for Leaving Homeland by Salawu Olajide
with a preface by Shara McCallum

Prodigal Daughter by Hiwot Adilow
with a preface by Mahtem Shiferraw

Undressing Under the Noon Sun by Charity Hutete
with a preface by Nick Makoha

You Too Will Know Me by Ama Asantewa Diaka
with a preface by Tjawangwa Dema

INTRODUCTION TO
SABA: NEW-GENERATION AFRICAN POETS,
A CHAPBOOK BOX SET
2020

Featured poets: Adedayo Adeyemi Agarau, Michelle K. Angwenyi, Afua Ansong, Fatima Camara, Sadia Hassan, Safia Jama, Henneh Kyereh Kwaku, Nadra Mabrouk, Nkateko Masinga, Jamila Osman, Tryphena Yeboah

Featured artist: Tariku Shiferaw

Introduction in Two Movements

Part One
Sankofa

I will not be so bold as to make claims about directions and thematic trends in African poetry today because, after all, I come to this introduction not as someone who has attempted a deep scientific survey, but rather someone who, for the past decade, has been privileged to read a great deal of poetry written by emerging poets from Africa. And what I can say is that, as with generations of poets before them, this current generation is contending with what can best be termed "modernity" in African culture. And whereas in the past, notions of migration, globalism, and cultural "clashes" were defined by communication that was less fluid, less accessible, and more expensive, the fact is that the superficial "borders" that separate our worlds are more porous because we are traveling more, and we are connecting across all sorts of forms of media in unprecedented ways.

In reading this year's iteration of the *New-Generation African Poets Chapbook Box Set*, I kept being drawn back to the idea of border crossings, of movement, and, in many instances, of migration. Many other common threads of form and content emerge in this work, but I thought it would be fruitful to consider this core notion of movement—a phenomenon that Toni Morrison, in her long essay *The Origin of Others* (2017), declared to be the most dominant theme of the twenty-first century. These African poets are confirming this.

In Jamila Osman's poem "Winter," a drama unfolds—it is a play, with scene-setting, characters, and stage directions. The setting is the Pearson International Airport in Toronto, Canada, and at the center of the drama is a Customs officer. These elements are quick clues into a theme and subject that seem to preoccupy the poets in this season of box sets. Again and again, the "border," the place of crossing, the discourses of departure and arrival, of flight, of loss, and the many meanings of home, seem to haunt poet after poet. Some engage the subject directly, while others only suggest, creating a context for the poems, whether they are written by poets fully located in Africa or by those who find themselves crossing back and forth between Africa and elsewhere, or between their home countries and other countries, whether in Africa or outside. Jamila Osman engages the language of migration and nationhood in her title (*A Girl Is a Sovereign State*), and much of the time she employs it as a source of metaphor for understanding the dynamics of gender, the politics of the body, and the practice of selfhood. In "Winter," she shows that all of this must be framed by an understanding of the politics of place, and the border is the grand symbol. And as with so many of the poems in these chapbooks, any exploration of place, migration, or home, is a discussion negotiated through family:

Scene 1:

Location: Toronto Pearson International Airport.
Outside snow softens the unfamiliar landscape, whittles the
 winter's sharp edge.
The Canadian flag flaps in the wind.

Characters: A scowling Customs official in full uniform. A
 wedding ring cutting into his finger.
A young woman with no bags, a slip of paper with a phone
 number in her sweaty palm.

Customs official: *Name?*
My girl-mother: *Refugee.*

It is a violent encounter not because anyone physically assaults the mother but because the language she uses—the words she speaks—is alien to her, and the cold is an assault on her body as it splits open her knuckles and lips.

And in "Girls, Girls, Girls," an elegy to innocence, a poem that addresses her awakening to the troubles in the world, makes clear that the true realities that will overthrow the innocence of girlhood are going to be about the violence with which the alien must contend. And so language is learned to manage the hardship of migration, and at the same time, and most beautifully, Osman connects this theme with her mother.

> Before we learned enough Arabic to perform the funeral prayer,
> Before the first body we mourned was our own.
>
> Before we came to know the geography of our mothers' grief,
> Before we contorted our bodies to fill the shape of her lost country.

For Osman the solution to the vicissitudes of immigration is found inside, it is found in the woman's ability to claim her own sovereignty, having been disappointed by other ways of defining identity: "The body of a girl / is a nation" she says, "with no flag / of its own." At the end of this title poem, she writes, "A girl is a sovereign state. / I will not be a stranger / here / or anywhere." I must admit that when I read a stanza like this, from Safia Jama's *Notes on Resilience,* I grow excited, hungry to read more:

> I was nineteen when my father
> took my picture somewhere near
> the Somali-Ethiopian border.

The reasons should be obvious enough, but they are worth rehearsing. The stanza suggests the value of history and memory—there is a suggestion that an intimacy is being wrestled with and explored. This is the power of the past tense, it is the trust engendered by the first person, and it does reflect the risk. That then, is the draw of time—the way it starts to demand an engagement that is guided by an intimate engagement with history. The second draw is place, and by place, we also mean time and history. So much is contained in the word "border" and even more in the uncertainty and danger of "somewhere near." So much about the geopolitics of Africa, so much about migration, so much about arrivals and departures. What is it that takes bodies to "the Somali-Ethiopian border," and what is being negotiated when a nineteen-year-old woman remembers this instant in which time is arrested and sealed into memory—a snapshot taken at a border where two nations are in conflict, at peace, or certainly trying to work through the divisions of nation, war, and politics. The poem is called "Two Sisters," and I am reminded of just why this present exploration of the intimate life of this continent becomes a point of great possibility and fulfillment for me. The next stanza is as alluring for its detail and its evocation of the tactile:

I stood frowning in a flowing dress,
red fabric loosely covering my hair.

Jama's poem is replete with the themes and ideas that are echoed throughout this box set. It is simply true that the poets collected here are negotiating, in the most sophisticated and revealing ways, themes of place, history, and transition. This may simply be a result of the peculiar intensity of travel and movement that is the way of the world now. Borders are the sites of war, of escape, of discovery, of ethnic divisions, and more hopefully, the sites of imagination remaking, of cross-fertilization, of the strange confluence of cultures and ideas and bodies.

Sadia Hassan has her own borders to traverse—in her case, the Kenya/Somali border—and she is engaged by the psychic and emotional implications of border crossings and the meaning of migration.

> In Kenya, I was the woman I had always been: Somali
> refugee, smuggling children yesterday
> and today, a baby goat.
> ("Sujui")

Indeed, for her there is a comic absurdity to it all, but what I am drawn to, again and again, is the terrain that she is opening up to us because of the immediacy of this conversation. Her poem "Smell the Season of Rain Well Before It Is Upon Us" gifts readers with yet another instant of great promise and possibility. So much is packed into a few lines:

> In Kenya, my body becomes a tuning fork. I arrive in the heat humming, thick with surrender. I heard God loves a good story and so I returned from the cold noise of America to repent in earnest for lonelying my mother, for leaving and leaving for College.

In poem after poem in this box set, the body figures (as it has in much poetry from Africa over the last few years) as the subject of rich study to any enterprising scholar who is interested in discovering intersections between sexuality, gender, alienation, and self-image and identity in African writing. Here, the body as "tuning fork" is a splendid metaphor to open the door to the poems collected here. Migration has a cost, and that cost, blessedly, is expressed fruitfully through the tuning bodies of these poets.

For Nkateko Masinga in her chapbook *Psalm for Chrysanthemums*, while the two destinations of travel she mentions in the book (namely, South Africa and the US, specifically Richmond, Virginia) are not the framing of the entire work, we find in her sense of arrival and departure a metaphor for the more centralized theme, that of emotional and psychological transport—migration and exile and the quest for home. Here, the geography of the South African landscape is her source of metaphor, and so are seasons, so are the names of plants. This is not pastoral verse; instead, these are poems that show the poet to be alive to a sense of place and the emotional value of such alertness:

> In my mania, I was the highveld
> with tall plateaus and rolling plains,
> too much hill to fit into this world.
> ("Inpatient")

And then in America, as a visitor, the alienness is the very pleasure of her experience of exile. She wants to be away. There is the odd ritual of fireworks in a country where war is honored and celebrated and in which war veterans struggle with PTSD. But rather than being traumatized by the fireworks of the fourth of July, she finds a comfort in the alienness of these rituals:

> My host mother asked if the fireworks would trigger me,
> if there were wars back home that sounded just like this
> and I said, 'I came here to forget what home sounds like.'
> ("My Lover Pulls Me Off the Train Tracks")

For Ghanian poet Tryphena Yeboah, the long discourse of her sequence of poems, tantalizingly titled *A Mouthful of Home*, is faith, belief, and religion, and the site for the contestation of this is the intimate relationship between mother, father, and daughter—a conversation of presence, absence, loss, and the discovery of new ways to understand the self as separate from the familial. It is all grounded in Ghana, in its geography, and yet these ideas of migration emerge. Yeboah, too, provides us with these gems about movement, which, though grounded in place, is hardly static, hardly locked to a singular moment.

> I TELL MY MOTHER I WANT A BODY THAT EXPANDS
> Into a map. She wants to know where I'll travel to. I say "myself."

For her, the journey to self is one that echoes the agenda of all poetry, it seems, but in her exploration of her mother, who figures significantly in these poems, the intimacy is refreshing for its generosity. And by this, I mean that in this openness to sharing her life, Yeboah is generous. In her poem "Honoring What My Family Will Never Know," she writes beautifully:

> Leaving opens us up,
> makes a keeper out of us,
> shows us we're made of more rooms
> than we can count.

This could easily be an epigraph for this collection, and it offers a striking line of examination for so much of what we are seeing in the poetry by the younger generation of African poets. What it reveals is that leaving never quite happens. In fact, leaving is a return, a return to the meaning of the self.

The Adinkra symbol of Akan civilization translates to "farewell," and, given its long association with funeral rituals, one need not think too hard to recognize that movement and transport of the body and the mind serve an elemental role in society. Afua Ansong's poems in her collection, *Try Kissing God*, allow her to have a conversation with the spirit world, one rooted in Ghanaian philosophy and spiritual beliefs even as they achieve a modernity about arrivals and departures that echoes the rest of these chapbooks.

In her poems, despite their being based in the Ghanaian cultural milieu, one has the sense of departure, as if the poems are all rehearsing the Sankofa symbol of departure and return. This opens the way for a wonderful dance between arrivals and departures, which, in the end, become defining markers of the meaning of "home."

> *if you want to be free you could stop picking,*
> *if you want to run, you can bury yourself,*
> *lie in the field of flowers, white and soft, your burial,*
> *until water pours out of your holes.*
>
> Mother, do not fear.
> The earth itself will drink our blood.
> ("ASASE YƐ DURU")

Ansong's two-worldness is endemic. It is not, in the Walcottian sense, an even divide, but it is a world in which "home" is interrupted and set in relief by "away." She calls her double-sightedness access to "the best of two worlds." Home, though, is found in her defiant hair—the Africanness of her hair.

> Blessed are those who bantu knot and oil massage their
>   scalps to sleep
> and rise with coconut oil stains on their pillows.

Blessed are the naturals that plead with dandruffs after a
   co-wash.
Blessed are you who transition and possess the best of two
   worlds.
Blessed are those who cut and cut until they turn into their
   roots.
("DUAFE")

And like hair, love is found in this awareness of difference in the poem "ODO NNYEW FIE KWAN" (which translates to "Love never loses its way home"). The lover is likely clandestine—he has a "girlfriend" who is not the speaker, and he is white. But even when he is with her, sharing a bed, he is able to sense her presence and absence. The idea is that love will find home, but the counter idea is that what is happening in the moment is not the "home" that dominates. That is the most haunting:

> You whisper *home is a song to the womb*
> into the green night, your slender fingers
> arched around his wanting ears.
> He tames your clay hands,
> lowers your fingers into his and replies
> *still you must return to it.*

Fatima Camara's familial conversation with the past, with history and with the present in her collection, *YellowLine,* is inextricably entwined with ideas of departure and arrival, or what she calls "landings." Underneath these discoveries of self, of personal histories and of the repetition of identity, is the looming idea of migration. It is elemental to the throughline of the work:

> I don't remember the first time I met my
> grandmother. I remember before the second
> time thinking there's no way this woman exists.
> We must think we know where to find her.
> This woman who's lost so much must be lost too.
> ("Prep")

Implicit in this "forgotten" meeting is the narrative of the speaker moving from the myth of a grandmother—one told to her by her mother and others—to meeting her. It is a striking meeting—one characterized by the fulsome and beautiful presence of the grandmother, who never, in these poems, is easily seen as a comfortable part of the speaker. There is a divide, one that Camara is constantly seeking to bridge with poetry, with language. And guiding this process of retrieval is the sea as a symbol of separation and movement.

> If you wanted to find the ones that have floated to
> shore,
> the survivors, all around there are plenty of other
> bodies
> that shine like mine.
> ("Sanno")

The image is hauntingly familiar—it evokes the bodies of refugees strewn on the beaches of Europe after the Mediterranean crossing. This is now a constant trope in much of the poetry and fiction of Africa. It is not an invention nor a fancy. Yet for Camara, there is another body of water, one she calls "the mid-Atlantic ridge," where she imagines her grandmother has died, where she has become "a seabed." Yet this death is a moment of reclamation and restoration:

My grandmother
is no longer
one who has met her end
but who has gone back to the beginning.

Till she is the seabed.
Till she is the land kicked back
to the surface.
("Erosion")

In her poem "Repetition," however, Camara lays out the deep-seated anxieties and complexities of familial divides caused by migration or the prospect of migration. These are not poems of geopolitical polemics, but these are poems that go further, that help us to see the consequences of migration:

She taught, I learned. We understand different.

> Two different countries, we move different.
> From where did you come, child? she asks.

Always the questions that aren't really asked.
From a woman whose body rejects this land.

> I scream that I didn't choose this landing.
> She screams that this land did not make me.

So I wait for her to recognize me.
We wake and in front of a mirror, we stand.

It is hopeful, this ending, this way in which the speaker recognizes herself in her mother's body, a body that is acutely alienated in a new land, a new "landing." These poems are a reclamation of an African self, one that is shaped and reimagined through language.

Henneh Kyereh Kwaku, of all the poets in this set, is most explicitly engaged with the wider world. His sardonic wit and cutting critique of postcolonial society constantly position the meaning of Ghana against what Ghana is not—the forces that are collapsing on Ghana and forcing the country to react. He is interested in the relationship between the cedi and the franc and the dollar. He is fully aware of the dangerous presence of the Chinese in West Africa and the compromises that are leading to this circumstance—the corruption and the desperation. While Kwaku is not explicitly engaged by migration as a trope of self and identity, his awareness of Ghanaian modernity within the wider world in his collection "Revolution of Scavengers," and its construction of a genuine global economy, puts into stark relief the meaning of nation, the meaning of self, and the meaning of cultural identity.

> I still don't understand why Ghana & Nigeria do not add up. *Sweat too na water abi?* Let the Chinese come for the bauxite at Atiwa & show us how to fetch sweat for distillation. *Na only sweat we dey get from the sun o, but we shun the solar energy. Or sweat be wonna solar energy?* Ra, we know—the God of the sun.
> ("Even in Our Differences There's a Similarity")

Kwaku, writing from the heart of the fulcrum, is fully aware of the ways in which the very notion of country, of flag, of sovereignty is constantly being contested by the circumstances of history. His postcolonial discourse is refreshing in the way it shakes up certain overused tropes that either seek to dismiss the persistence of colonialism and imperialism, or that remain fixated on those two forces as the sole arbiters of African destruction. Instead, Kwaku reminds us that nothing is that simple. A new discourse, for example, has to operate around the Chinese. In the poem "In This Mine We Pray," he asks, "Is it xenophobic to protect my water from Chinese miners?" These are tough questions, and poetry allows him to venture there:

> Do not take yourself from the action & say: *they took GH₵ 1.00 from me*. Say: *I bribed the police*. Blame yourself. Do not say our flag does not dance when between the French & the American flag—our flag is cotton & shy, not just anything blows it away—so was this country made. This is your country. Our flag is not on any missile meant to wipe half of the world—our presidents are not Thanos to snap & wipe. We'd rather snap & get Noah's Ark for Accra before the floods.
> ("Anything for the Boys?")

In poem after poem, what grows increasingly clear in Kwaku's work is that much of what is to be understood about Ghana, about Accra and its vulnerability to floods and drought, is as much defined by what happens in the country as it is by what happens outside. In a revealing and deeply honest anecdote in the poem "Welcoming a Ghanaian God," Kwaku offers an indirect but critical commentary on migration and the ways in which the definition of migrant is as important to those who have been left behind as it is to those who have left:

About a month ago, Kofi Kingston became WWE's first African-born world champion, his mother says he's a full Ghanaian. Not African-American. Not Ghanaian-American—he's not hyphenated. He's full. She makes me believe again that being Ghanaian is something to be proud of.

Egyptian poet Nadra Mabrouk is a woman in transition between cultures in her chapbook *Measurements of Holy*. But like so many of the poets in this set, the most vital stage for the enactment of the drama of migration is the relationship between the mother and the daughter.

> My mother on the phone
> is upset that I still remember her sitting
> on the kitchen floor of her mother's
> apartment in Shobra, plucking feathers
> from the mottled bodies of geese, their insides
> jeweled and engorged on their own shimmering,
> their necks hanging over her wrists
> like unclasped bracelets.
> ("Autumn, Spiraling")

Her mother is the connection to memory and to Cairo. It is a connection to childhood, and it is a troubled and uncertain memory because it is associated with the divide between home and what is not home, or what has become another home. Importantly, what the poet remembers, the image of her mother plucking goose feathers, is an image that upsets her mother. Mabrouk does not explain why. She merely leaves this negotiating between memory and the present as a point of rupture and uncertainty.

Thus in her poem "Portrait of the Country in Which I Was Born," that country is a child and at the same time a body, not unlike the lost mother who resists memory, resists being reduced to a memory by being an unruly memory. In a striking image, Mabrouk locates one of the core dilemmas of migration—the fact that the "home place," or the place of contested origin, is not a static place, even if it feels that way in memory. The poet is frustrated by the subject who simply won't keep still:

> We can barely hear anything now over this display,
>
> desperate for memory, I need you to hold still so that we
>   may get this right.
> Here is a knife, I will be quicker this time. I will even sing you
>   a song.

The collection is soaked in a haunting sense of loss, not merely within the poet herself, but also in those around her, and especially in the parents. It may seem obvious enough to point this out, but it is worth reflecting on the extent to which so many of these poets recognize the dilemmas of movement—even in the prospect of otherness, of simply looking outside of home from home, for the security and stability of "home" which is being threatened and tested. In the beautiful portrait of her father as a young man in Egypt, Mabrouk imagines the father's departure before it happens:

> how your mother was crying
> of a dream in which the hand

of every person you ever loved
was reaching for you from a river
whose current surged, their fingers swelling
in the progress, palms barely recognizable,
African tigerfish swarming again and again.
("Father as Adolescent, Smoking")

Adedayo Adeyemi Agarau in *The Origin of Name* offers us a sense of what happens when a poet insists on the quest for a grounding in "home," in tradition and in the rituals of an ancient culture in the face of modernity. Indeed, as if in response to the turmoil and upheaval of travel, movement, and alienation from home, Agarau presents a meditation on the importance of having a grounding in the spiritual practices of the society as a preparation to travel, to venture outside of home. It is this grounding that allows movement to be possible.

The gods ask us to bring salt and sprinkle it on this soil,
    to beckon earth mothers to rise from flames,
to give us dreams wide enough to ferry us,
    to build us a boat and name each land a city across the sea,
give us feathers and wings and letters and names.
("The Gods Ask Us to Make an Oasis")

In his poem "Bantale Drowning in the Flower Room," Agarau is clearly thinking of those who are exiled aliens living in society and those from "home" who have left and are living in exile. Without commenting on the ethical or even political implications of exile, he observes narratives of travel, of exile—narratives that we have seen have captured the imagination of so many of the poets included here; rather than merely speaking to the hardships of travel, of migration and movement, they offer a reminder of the value of "home." It is this seeming contradiction that permeates the work we encounter here:

> Perhaps each of your exiles
> is a reminder that home
> is the paradise of woods.

Michelle K. Angwenyi's poems are careful internal quarrels—the world outside of the mind, the working through of the self that is muted except when she is constructing a sense of place as a way to understand feeling and thought. The title of her collection, *Gray Latitudes,* invokes ideas of geography and place. But in the poems, she is employing these ideas in largely metaphorical ways—the latitudes represent the lines that separate what is understood and what she is wrestling to understand. Yet in her first poem, "Memorial," the language of travel, of arrivals and departures, is employed in ways that align with the work of other poets in the series:

> These are the elaborate one-sided goodbyes.
> The learning to accept tea from strangers.
> The voiceless convergence of winds.
>
> —
>
> . . .
>
> The slowness of arrival. The always arriving.
> The day, and its salt pillars.
> And the sun, still water.

In the one poem that names her home city and offers a striking and evocative portrait of the city, Angwenyi reminds us that often "home" is understood best in juxtaposition to what it is not.

> In this place of colliding times,
> no word for it in childhood, and unrecognizable in this dusk,
> Nairobi comes and goes.
> I had the word for it yesterday,
> and the need that follows, to remember that
> feeling:
> too-long trousers, newspaper kites, lost boys
> and now, grown-up absences via the labyrinths of other cities.
> ("Part II: Gray Latitudes")

Nairobi, described as a place of "colliding times," is indeed a city with a relative history of hosting many interlopers and of various cultures imposing on Kikuyu and Massai land. During the nineteenth century, the city was at the heart of all the great changes in that country—all the collisions of people and movements. Yet the Nairobi she speaks of here is elusive and changeable, which is part of its beauty. In the end, its meaning is found in the "absences," the movement of people from Nairobi to "other cities." It is in this sense that Angwenyi reflects what Patricia Jabbeh Wesley says in her introduction to the chapbook. She sees in Angwenyi, and by extension in the new generation of African poets, a refreshing new possibility:

> *Gray Latitudes* defies all norms by navigating the modern literary landscape of the African at home and abroad—a new domain that invites us all to write our

Africa in its complete modernity and tradition, whatever that is in the new world.

—*Kwame Dawes*

Part Two
The Horse of Language

When you are engaged primarily in facilitating the production of a yearly curated list of books, you are engaged with the frenetic energy that comes with it—deadlines, negotiation, fundraising, and the never-ending process of selecting, editing, and juxtaposing books like tracks on an old-school EP. In the matrix of that kind of energy, it is hard to contend with big-picture matters like trends, canons, or even the journey so far. For that, editors have to rely on critical readers, scholars, and other poets.

Appropriately, Kwame has chosen the Akan word *Sankofa* as the title for his section of the introduction. A deeply West African word, Sankofa is simultaneously a word, a proverb, a symbol, an Adrinka ideograph that implies (please note that I have chosen not to say "means;" I chose the word implies because almost every word in any West African language—and this includes names—is an elision of complex ideas and stories so that we can only imply the possibilities it is addressing) a kind of looking back in order to move forward. A sort of curatorial review.

And in keeping with the spirit of Sankofa, the insights he gleans serve only as general signposts on an ongoing journey but never claim any singular authority on knowing. Always it is about a gleaning, an implying. In a way these introductions have come to be simultaneous conversations between Kwame and me, the editors and the readers, the whole list of the African Poetry

Book Fund and a kind of Western Canon, the editors and the poets (not only those we have published but those we are yet to publish). They are conversations with the wider world of African scholarship, with the tradition, and with an African artistic and philosophical worldview. Communicating the complexity of these negotiations in just a few words requires us to write clearly, definitively even, but open-ended.

Proverbs, the distillation of a complex wisdom to an image, is as complex in human thought as a quantum entanglement. In Yoruba, a proverb, Owe, is called the horse language rides. In other words, the implication is that language is not a fixed system of meaning as we are often taught to think of it in Western (or should I say modern capitalist?) thought. As we say in my small town of origin, Afikpo, language is a river that flows toward the future carrying the knowledge of before into the possibility of now. One can think of a poem, a prayer, a song, or even just an exclaimed sound as a proverb—the horse that all the ineffable hopes of our human self rides in language, a gesture always fluttering in time and space. Poetry has as its central concern language itself. Language and its slippery forms. It feels sometimes that in all African languages there is more fluidity in the articulations of self than in the languages that are more deeply mired in the transactions of capital. I am not pointing to any primitivism here in thought or scholarship (because these languages are more complex than current Western forms) but only stating that precisely because these languages haven't been at the heart of global capitalism, they haven't been reduced to a mere transactional state. They hold simultaneity and occasional convergence with ease, having no need to fall into either side of one single transaction.

African thought, particularly West African thought (and the

expression of such in dense forms is the proverb), visualizes life and all its attendants as the concept of journey, of travel. So many proverbs are expressions of travel in time, space, and conceptualization. Here are a few to think about: to get lost is to learn the way; by crawling a child learns to stand; by trying often the monkey learns to jump from the tree; nobody is born wise; you learn to cut down trees by cutting them down; you don't teach the paths of the forest to an old gorilla; traveling is learning. I could go on ad infinitum. We see the ideas of presence as a doubling back, but also as a moving forward in time, space, width, length, and breadth and interiority. These are at the heart of our linguistic DNA as Africans, and therefore the composition of our worldview, which is that of convergence and multiplicity. In other words, time (and therefore all measurable phenomena) becomes, as the Yoruba say, La-Lai, or, as the Igbo say, Akile—an entanglement. At once converging into a "moment" before fracturing into simultaneity. Even the rituals of Africa are designed as a journey—even the construction of prayers and proverbs—and so it follows that poems are made from this deeply embedded matrix, and they must therefore carry these dimensionalities inside them.

So, then, we ask what does any of that have to do with this chapbook box set? Well, everything and maybe nothing. Perhaps you will have to be the judge of that. But here is the thing, the bulk of the work we are reading is grouped around the idea of identity. Surely everything is, you might say. But in this case the identity explored is different and specific. There was a time within African life and thought that identity involved distancing ourselves from the colonial oppression that had lasted on the continent for, in some cases, well over a hundred years and also indirectly, for another three hundred before that, by way of destructive commerce with the Portuguese and the British, and also of course with the trade in humans as slaves.

The identity that was forged through postcolonialism was national rather than more humanist or even modernist. Such identities became essentialized very quickly. So much of what we think of as identity was assumed and conflated with nation and forged in response to Western incursion. We seldom came to these modern—or perhaps a better word is recent—selves in the modern literatures post-independence via a slow accretion of a modernist arc. We instead assumed common constructed selves (so constructed in response to whiteness and heterosexual patriarchy; after all, the nation was the all Father) and wrote in "epic" voices that addressed in bombast. We were mainly praise singers chanting big songs in support of a shaky, often unquestioned, essential identity. In very much the same way that masculinity is forged in a series of evacuated negatives (as in, I am a man because I am not . . . and we return to this and fathers later), this new identity, and even the poetics of its address, was constructed in the same way. The flow and flex of a poetics in flux, journey and uncertainty of language and the mediation of self via the multiplicities articulated above, gave way to this new misconstrued "modern" approach. Almost a propaganda of what we were and were not. The journey at the heart of identity via language as ritual, as the vehicle of the ineffable, was suppressed. In that context, the novel, already seen as the vehicle of identity and nation in the West, took leadership. Poetry, and the gift of slippage and question, got lost in the mix or took the form of verse masking the heart of prose. We see this still to a large extent in contemporary American poetry.

As Kwame points out, immigration is considered the pressing issue of the twenty-first century, and he gestures toward Toni

Morrison's beautiful take on it in her book *The Origin of Others* (and we are aware that there are many other examples that could have been cited). And while it is true that migration/immigration—forced (and much of it is about displacement, loss, and poverty) and voluntary (better deployment of skills and abilities, etc.)—is at the cutting edge of the century, it's not true that it is new or a sudden phenomenon (not that Kwame is arguing that it is). We are all familiar with the fear and expression of the barbarians at the gate. The unique challenges of this century are scale (the sheer numbers are overwhelming), the privilege of host populations that place immigrant populations at a disadvantage educationally and with fewer skill sets, the neglected pressures of climate change and the impact on resources, the unchecked capitalism and the ever-growing gulf between those who have and don't have, and many more such pressures mean that the patterns of movement and the direction of flow is overwhelmingly one-directional. So then, in the new flex, we finally have to contend with assertions like those by Homi Bhabha that "identity is not a destination, it's a state of flux," as visceral realities and not just mental and academic jumps in conceptual territories while bodies remain static (sometimes with the fixed essential identities mentioned before). Whatever else the anxieties might be, this provides real and exciting opportunities for discovery within African literature. With novels still locked so heavily in place defending long-since-defunct territories (this does not of course include exciting forms like speculative fiction and sci-fi, to name just two), poetry can, with its innate ability to shape narratives while not being married to the sequential flow of time and space, step up to ask and explore the resulting questions.

In these new poetic forms and voices, we find that the essential identities of the past fall easily away, and the loss that we are left with gives rise to the need for more individual and nuanced explorations resulting in the proliferation of negotiations that Kwame so elegantly and effortlessly lays bare in his section, relying entirely on the work as an evidentiary offering—and what a rich one it is. This quest here is a form of modernism, but a form that is not what we are used to thinking of, which is a modernist approach in relation to Western philosophy, which positions itself as the next real jump after that so wrongly named age of enlightenment. This, what we encounter here, is a return to that much more complex and advanced philosophy of self that the African past offers. Our languages of expression and the ideas behind them, even via the colonial oppressions of English, French, Spanish, and Portuguese remain in flux, fluid and flexible, waiting for new horsemen and horsewomen to ride it into the twenty-first century. Hold that thought.

That many of these poets reside in the diaspora is not a limitation but a necessity because the truth is that the continent of Africa is a complex negotiation of internal diasporas. Hausas range from Senegal through Nigeria and into Cameroon. Yorubas from Western Nigeria through to Sierra Leone, and the same for Igbos. In fact some scholars argue that the idea of a Yoruba nation results in smaller nations expanding into empires and occupying territories that held other nations. And they go further to argue that the word Yoruba is from the ethnic nation of Nupe, bordering the old Oyo empire, and is a Nupe word that means "those people." So, where else to make sense of a fractured identity than in cultures, and places where there is so much pressure on essentialism that questions that could not be asked at home must be confronted abroad? Remember the Yoruba and Lai-Lai? It's all an entanglement, and the very least of it is that we come back to the original horse of language, the home of self. Hold that thought.

For a long time, Kwame and I were trying to encourage a very particular African poetics to develop. We have tried to allow this evolution to happen as organically as we can. We have nudged scholars, poets, and even reviewers to consider this angle, but of all the demographics, it is the poets themselves who have generated the general outlines of a distinctly African Poetics through the variety and strength of the work itself. So in this chapbook box set, the eighth in the series, and nearly 100 chapbooks in, we are finally seeing not so much a trend or trends but a deep struggle to figure out what African literary Modernism can be. We are seeing the true articulation of identity from multiple points of view, rather than an embrace or push away from an essential monolithic identity—a conversation generated, sustained, and trusted outside of simple binaries and whose textual referents are generated in the process and not from already existing ideological positions. A way forward, a new horse of language.

—Chris Abani

The Chapbooks of
Saba: New-Generation African Poets, A Chapbook Box Set

Enumeration by Sadia Hassan
with a preface by Matthew Shenoda

A Girl Is a Sovereign State by Jamila Osman
with a preface by Ladan Osman

Gray Latitudes by Michelle K. Angwenyi
with a preface by Patricia Jabbeh Wesley

Measurement of Holy by Nadra Mabrouk
with a preface by Karen McCarthy Woolf

A Mouthful of Home by Tryphena Yeboah
with a preface by Lauren K. Alleyne

Notes on Resilience by Safia Jama
with a preface by Hope Wabuke

The Origin of Name by Adedayo Adeyemi Agarau
with a preface by Mahtem Shiferraw

Psalm for Chrysanthemums by Nkateko Masinga
with a preface by Shara McCallum

Revolution of the Scavengers by Henneh Kyereh Kwaku
with a preface by Henk Rossouw

Try Kissing God by Afua Ansong
with a preface by Romeo Oriogun

YellowLine by Fatima Camara
with a preface by Honorée Fanonne Jeffers

INTRODUCTION TO
NANE: NEW-GENERATION AFRICAN POETS, A CHAPBOOK BOX SET
2021

Featured poets: Kolawole Samuel Adebayo, Cynthia Amoah, Precious Arinze, Lameese Badr, Sara Elkamel, Edil Hassan, Jeremy Teddy Karn, Hauwa Shaffii Nuhu, Selina Nwulu, Ayan M. Omar, Saradha Soobrayen, Ajibola Tolase, Qutouf Yahia

Featured artist: Admire Kamudzengerere

Introduction

Despite the steady regularity—the ritual, even—of putting together this series, we remain deeply impressed by what has been produced and the work we see emerging season after season. This project demands steady focus and a curiosity about what African poets are writing these days. We began with the determination that, at least for the first decade of this series, we would not seek to construct or even signal an artistic manifesto or a guide that could be construed as prescriptive—a functional manifesto, if you will, of what *should* be African poetry. Instead, we determined that our posture would be one of deep curiosity, a desire to let the work teach us something of the state and nature of African poetry, or, better put, of poetry written by Africans.

Chris Abani observed very early in the process that a symbiotic phenomenon had started to manifest in the poetry we were seeing year after year. The observation remains vital today—having observed it once, it is now impossible to avoid. Poets are reading other poets and are in dialogue with them. This is not a unique thing, but it is worthy of remark in African poetry today because of how much this "conversation" is helping to shape a discourse.

Each year, we get to look at the work of several hundred poets through the Sillerman First Book Prize entries, and then beyond that, we also ask for recommendations from writers, arts administrators, and editors across Africa and the diaspora. We have a long-standing relationship with the Brunel International African Poetry Prize, and so are given access to some of the top work that its judges identify. We look at this work and end up with an even stronger sense of what is taking shape with African poets. It is always true that as a movement starts to swell, there is a great deal of "conversation" going on between poets that can be intentional or completely unintentional. Much of it is driven by the evidence of success—of publication—and some of it is the wonderful sense among poets who are isolated by geography, who lack evidence that poets in their position can have success, that they are not alone, and that they can be ambitious and discover their voice. There is the splendid enlivening that happens when one reads poets who write about familiar subjects, landscapes in which they live. And even when, across various countries in Africa, they recognize the difference, the strangeness of the writer's culture, they find a way to translate that strangeness into a belief in the fitness of their own landscape, their own history, their own culture, for poetry. We can see that this does not always lead to fully developed poetry, but it leads to a wave of language that is writing into being a shifting culture, a world that is complex and dynamic. It has become harder to avoid describing this intense "seeing" as a function of modernity in all its complexity, and in all the ways that it speaks to the past, present, and future.

This conversation is extremely important because it reminds us that the idea of a poetic community enacts the promise of being seen. There is a sense in which this community is virtual. Of course, in this realm the pattern is not entirely strange or new. The formation of an entity called "African literature" was occasioned by certain physical proximities between artists. Bright and gifted colonials, moving to the United Kingdom to be educated at the major British universities, created communities of "immigrants" who would become a cadre of anticolonials because their meeting and their conversation revealed to them the sophisticated conspiracy of exploitation that constituted the British Empire. Members of the empire were talking to each other, recognizing themselves in each other, and soon planning their liberation. Yet not all postcolonial African writers migrated. Many discovered the other postcolonial from around the world through an earlier version of the virtual—the book. This version had its limitations, not the least of which was speed. In necessary ways, technology was continuing its ancient work of constructing an urgent sense of modernity. None of this has changed.

So, there is something exciting happening in this virtual moment. Where the previous generations of poets needed the body to be present before intellectual negotiations could effectively take place, this new generation seems to be free from that. It is something worth aspiring to, because most of the violence and limitations of the twentieth century were seemingly caused by problems of the body. Whose body is this? Why is it here? Does it have a right to be here? Etc., etc., etc. In a way, this virtual space allows for more free-flowing conversation across ethnic, racial, aesthetic, political, and even, one can argue, spiritual lines. These poets are beginning negotiations around the body leaning into a citizenship that is more global, whose allegiances are not to communities of passport necessarily, but more communities of identification, a genuinely more modernist exploration of self. The outcome is a new poetic possibility, and a new set of dialogues.

This also overcomes some of the difficulties we face in Africa and African writing as a whole. There are many linguistic limitations to community in Africa. Particularly a literary community, which would suggest access to shared languages in print. There has never been much money in printing books on the continent; even in modern publishing complexes we have seen a reduction in the amount of success. Consider: Africa has Arabic to the north and east; English, French, and Spanish to the west; Portuguese, English, and more to the south; and thousands of indigenous languages across the board. Then there's the matter of literacy within these linguistic groups. If you have a continent like this, the problems of translation and access—exacerbated by economics, population, and landmass—become almost unsolvable. How, then, can there be "African literature" when we are not all literate in the linguistic modes of its varied production? How, then, can there be influence or dialogue if we cannot speak to or read each other?

Enter the Internet. It allows people to share publications digitally, bypass perceived or real gatekeepers, editors and other curators of material. It allows for simultaneous translations, for the distribution of translations with minimal cost. Case in point: a recent experiment (*Jalada Africa*'s translation project) that allowed a story by Ngugi wa Thiong'o, originally written in Gikuyu, to go viral in over fifty languages simultaneously. The Internet allows poets who are used to sharing work online, and who are not so bothered by the limits of intellectual property and its control, to share content and ideas through mobile phones, scanned images, and other media. People have a sense of what is being rewarded and how it's being rewarded and how people are finding spaces to express themselves. This virtual community has been part of the shaping of the African Poetry Book Fund and the chapbook series from the beginning, and if we were to be honest, these remarkable publishing enterprises, ambitiously seeking to create a massive network of poets across a massive continent and its diaspora, would be impossible otherwise. The APBF has been at work for seven years, and its most active, intimate, and dynamic editorial board has never physically met as a group!

When we first went on poetry tours across the continent, we saw vibrant communities engaged in production, sharing, and trading. What they lacked was archiving and access to more global spaces of visibility and engagement. Enter the African Poetry Book Fund and its many engagements. Unlike Heinemann's African Writers Series, which was edited by Chinua Achebe and later Abdulrazak Gurnah (a more controlled curation), we have allowed much of the content to do its own negotiation, find its own way, create its own clusters and constellations. This community is beautiful and flourishing and can finally see itself across generations (sometimes) and within the same generation, which has increased the conversations around linguistic forms and practices and advanced the aesthetic dramatically. In other words, African poets of this generation see and engage with each other unlike any other generation before. What has emerged is a common ideology that developed not from the outside voice of critics but from the actual creators of this imaginative scholarship, the poets themselves. That is why we endeavor to archive, collect, and curate always with a respectful distance, always with an understanding that we come here to learn, not to shape.

African poets of a certain generation are seeing each other. They have not named a school of poetics, nor have we seen a manifesto, but they are reading each other, they are "talking" to each other through the performative gestures of social media. They are also reading each other in the books that more slowly get around. These conversations are manifesting themselves in the poems we encounter on a regular basis. Enterprising poets have turned to imitation as a form of apprenticeship, while others have borrowed themes and poetic approaches as a pragmatic way of trying to make the case for why they should be published like their models have been. It is a sign that there is a lively dialogue taking place, that there is enough derivation to suggest that a vibrant and productive movement is happening. Derivation does not always lend itself to strong poetry, but it very often means that an individual talent is on their way toward a kind of originality. The impulse is a good one. The crisis of "voice" eventually leads to the recognition of the limitations of imitations, and finally—work having opened itself up to the self—freshness and power emerge.

Yet it is necessary to delve more deeply into this idea of derivation, for the case must be made that the presence of derivation is a sign of great health in a poetry community, something between mimicry, mimesis, and intervention. Perhaps the real thing lies in the word *derivation*. It evokes the notion of that which is derivative. But there is a key difference between derivation and that which is derivative, and that lies in the approach. A derivation is a creative practice: one comes to something, sees the use of a form as a container, as a guide, as a road map, and uses said cartography to position and channel new ideas and new possibilities—reggae is such a thing. That which is derivative is simply imitation with no new intervention. It is creative bankruptcy. There is nothing useful in it; there is no vision.

The key to this understanding can be found in the ways in which colonial language forms like English have been used within Africa. English—which has very strict rules, syntax, and grammar in its original home context—is seen as malleable, its rules of expression and use merely pointers, perhaps to guide conversation, to allow that which exists in indigenous thought, expression, and creativity to find form in a liminal space. This is why there are so many Englishes within West Africa alone. No one can hear any of these Englishes and think they are derivative. They are not derivative. They are artistic interventions, innovations, endlessly expanding, within the system of English but with permeable borders. There is something intrinsically syncretic, it seems, in West African and even larger African creative endeavor. Artists traveled and transported meme, forms and aesthetic philosophies and practices, down to idiomatic expressions. One can argue that indigenous languages like Yoruba and Igbo employ gestural movements that are embodied and three-dimensional. When such an imagination turns itself to derive something it cannot be derivative. So, we mean here that derivation is part of the way in which a new artistic practice is engaged in, creating energy, drive, and integrity.

These poets have inspired a new interest in their unspoken movements, which is why Western poets are constantly challenged and invigorated every time they encounter the poets or the work.

In this box set, there are many examples of poets "dialoguing" with other poets from Africa. They quote other poets, they dedicate poems to other poets, and they include epigraphs from other poets. And this is a promising indication that these poets are at least starting to conjure a "tradition," even if, at the moment, the dominant dialogue is with each other.

What is largely absent (with a few exceptions) is dialogue with the African poetry tradition that goes back four or five decades, not to mention traditions dating centuries. For the most part, one could not discern from the poetry of this new generation a body of work by African poets who came before. One does wonder what the reason for this might be. Many of the historically important African poets are no doubt taught in high school. But according to the poets we have been in touch with, the libraries have not always been good about prioritizing African poetry acquisitions or the formation of a collection. And this is further complicated by the fact that, despite the existence of such a body of work, there is an absence of institutions in which accomplished poets can formally train students, depriving poets in Africa of access to tradition. Of course, it is presumptuous of us to assume that this silence is borne of ignorance. It may well be a choice: perhaps these poets see no immediate connection between their own work and that of tradition.

The African Poetry Book Fund has not only been interested in recruiting new voices, but has also been aware of the value of intergenerational dialogue. As such, we have sought to establish an archive that tracks as much as possible, and keeps in print as much as possible, important African poets. Side by side with these box sets are the Sillerman First Book Prize books and the periodic release of work from our elders such as Kofi Awoonor, Keorapetse Kgositsile, Gabriel Okara, and Ama Ata Aidoo. One of our exciting new publications is a brilliant anthology of generation-spanning Sudanese poetry. This is exactly the kind of dialogue we hope to engender. We also try to acquire and print midcareer poets too. The idea is to make available enough of a generational conversation to bring back into relevance things that may have dropped away—not only for the public's engagement but also for the practitioners themselves.

Of course, since we are publishing individual creative imaginations, we cannot provide access to this material for free and the given material conditions of Africa limit access to a mass market for books. But we are trying to address with other means soon to be announced. This is a battle being fought on many fronts, and we hope that, in time, the next generation will start to edit with us simultaneously and later step in when we eventually step back. We aim to create a self-sustaining machine that operates to preserve not only the dialogue but the archive itself.

One of the important implications for this outpouring of work is how it affects the landscape of African poetry. The fact is that African poetry has never waned in its presence over the years. Poets have been performing work in various contexts, and the growth of clubs, societies, and festivals has been steady and responsive to the various means of performance facilitated by the Internet. In Cape Town, the Badilisha Poetry X-Change has captured the power and vibrancy of poetry performance through their remarkable website, which has been in operation for over a decade as perhaps one of the most impressive and useful repositories of African poetry and poets in the world. From early on, they understood the value of the text on the page and the voice recorded, and the website featured performances of poetry in multiple languages and in multiple contexts. Of similar, though not equal, value remains the Poetry International Rotterdam website, which has been steadily building a catalog of African poets, one garnered from the poets invited to perform at that festival each year, but also from some special events that have spotlighted particular African traditions. Rotterdam has found ways to locate and feature African poets without relying on the publishing system. The danger, however, has been that such festivals have depended on African poets to enliven their events and to keep up with the wave of spoken-word performance, which was so dominant at one point that massive wars between stage and page were being waged in literary circles the world over. Unfortunately, this tendency to stereotype and limit the African poet to "performance" has hampered their standing within the economy of world poetry, in which status, access, and the longevity of careers is predicated, for better or worse, on the publishing industry. Were it true that African poets had not been publishing their work for centuries, one could argue that instead of succumbing to the "Western" business of publication, African poets should create their own economy of performance. The fact is that across the African continent and within its diaspora, the publishing of poetry has been as integral to its history as performance. In short, any genuine engagement with African poetry should appreciate that the expression of this poetic tradition is complex and manifests itself in myriad ways. That the poetry of Africa has emerged as all poetry emerges in all societies and cultures: through the dynamic of cultural dialogue, and through the varied ways in which language has survived and thrived.

These box sets, and the broader project of the African Poetry Book Fund, seek to ensure that the poetry of Africans, written as part of the long tradition of published poetry in Africa, is published and distributed and celebrated. We have steadily created an extensive anthology that reflects broadly and increasingly the range of poetry coming out of Africa. This season, we are especially pleased about the inclusion of work from Liberia and Mauritius.

We have been scrupulous about trusting the poets we encounter to teach us something about the poetics that seems to be emerging from Africa and its diaspora. The brilliant and generous poets who have been writing the prefaces for these box sets have also begun to point to some of the ways these poets are chronicling our moment.

This growing body of work is making new demands on the African poetry world. In time, the question of distribution and the availability of poetry books across Africa will have to be addressed. But, of equal importance is the necessary act of grappling with this work, with what these poets are saying and how they are doing what they are doing. Who are these poets paying attention to, who are they embracing, who are they challenging, who are they celebrating? They are drawing on oral traditions, proverbial traditions, the sophisticated exploration of many languages, the historical realities behind their art, and the tyranny of the present moment—the news, if you will. These poets are opening up landscapes that are reconsidering the philosophical implications of modernity, of sexuality, of faith, of beauty, of landscape. And as we explore these paths of influence and dialogue, we are indeed unearthing evidence of originality, the peculiar, unpredictable mapping of the personal in these works. In their defiantly distinctive voices, these poets are laying the groundwork for how we speak of Africa and African. And urgent work is needed to contend with these exciting matters of prosody.

We salute the poets and poems featured in this new box set.

—Kwame Dawes & Chris Abani

The Chapbooks of
Nane: New-Generation African Poets, A Chapbook Box Set

bitter, and sweet by Ayan M. Omar
with a preface by Phillippa Yaa de Villiers

Dugsi Girl by Edil Hassan
with a preface by Safiya Sinclair

Dust to Dust by Lameese Badr
with a preface by Samiya Bashir

Field of No Justice by Sara Elkamel
with a preface by Shara McCallum

Handrails by Cynthia Amoah
with a preface by Nathalie Handal

The Hope of Floating Has Carried Us So Far by Precious Arinze
with a preface by Parneshia Jones

In Her Deepest Sleep, Madam Lisette Talate Returns to Chagos
by Saradha Soobrayen
with a preface by Cheswayo Mphanza

Invocations by Kolawole Samuel Adebayo
with a preface by Rachel Eliza Griffiths

Keep the Bodies Buried by Selina Nwulu
with a preface by Honorée Fanonne Jeffers

Koola Lobitos by Ajibola Tolase
with a preface by Chekwube Danladi

Miryam Magdalit by Jeremy Teddy Karn
with a preface by Patricia Jabbeh Wesley

My Poets Don't Die by Qutouf Yahia
with a preface by Safia Elhillo

Sister by Hauwa Shaffii Nuhu
with a preface by 'Gbenga Adeoba

INTRODUCTION TO
TISA: NEW-GENERATION AFRICAN POETS,
A CHAPBOOK BOX SET
2023

Featured poets: Samuel A. Adeyemi, Nikitta Dede Adjirakor, O-Jeremiah Agbaakin, Rabha Ashry, Hazem Fahmy, Alain Jules Hirwa, Jay Kophy, Tawiah Naana Akua Mensah, Phodiso Modirwa, Nneoma Veronica Nwogu, Jakky Bankong-Obi

Featured artist: Victor Ekpuk

Introduction in Two Movements

Part One

Every year, Chris Abani and I find ourselves returning to a core question that forces us to consider the state of African poetry. The year is typically spent considering where things were when we started to think about an enterprise like the African Poetry Book Fund, and where we are now. In many ways, every new box set offers us a moment to think about what Africans are doing in poetry and where things are with the publishing of African poets. In this sense, the ritual of reviewing the manuscripts of emerging African poets is refreshing, for it affirms that Africans have never stopped finding ways to exist through the making of poems, the speaking of poems, and the business of contending with our lived world through language and the sharing of poetry. When this current box set appears, we will have published over 100 poets from Africa and of African descent in the space of eight years. Each year, the list of poets we approach for recommendations of emerging poets doing interesting work grows and spreads farther and farther around the continent and outside of it.

This is exciting. It does represent possibility. And rather than dwell on the sad state of affairs that would lead to a project like this having such an impact so quickly, I certainly would rather dwell on the beautiful ways in which African poetry is appearing in so many places where it was once quite rare. Here in the US, more and more African poets are being published by mainstream publishers and in many literary journals. They are winning awards, and they are developing their own communities and movements of poetry—organizing anthologies, creating websites, creating their own literary journals and much else—in ways that speak to the increased impact of the work we are doing. Many of the poets who are engaged in this work, and whose work we see appearing around the country and in the UK, are poets we published first in our chapbook series, or poets who were finalists in the Evaristo African Poetry Prize, the Sillerman First Book Prize for African Poets, and in various anthologies that we have published. But the APBF has effectively sought to expand its work in as organic a manner as possible. We recently received a generous grant from the Poetry Foundation to study poetry book distribution in Africa, venturing into an area of publishing that is not often studied, and about which we do not ask the difficult questions.

We are publishing poets, but is their work getting around? African publishers are publishing African poets, but does their work have a chance to be distributed to festivals, booksellers, bookstores, and libraries in Africa? We have hunches, but we don't know, and so we will try to find out. We are also pushing hard to create a landscape in which the poets we have collected here will thrive—an ecosystem that ensures that their work is received, studied, preserved, shared, and valued during their lifetime and long after they have gone. We have to think in this way. It is this idea, this impetus for a living archive. It is a deliberate act of affirming the long tradition of poetry from Africa and in finding ways to consider that its evolving and transformative present moment must be accounted for and preserved. We are also deeply aware of the fact that much of what we are doing now finds us navigating these matters in English. We are aware that what constitutes African poetry in English is a mere fraction of possibility when we consider the presence of poetry in Africa in the past and now. So, we have already began our work on translation and on offering what we can to start us all thinking about poetry in African languages, even as we embrace the notion (normally attributed to Achebe) that English, and French, and Portuguese, and Spanish, etc. are African languages. In this sense, we have a catholic view of things, embracing the idea that the whole conception of Africa and Africanness is one that is constantly evolving, and one that is profoundly and radically expanding. In this sense, the work we do is radical in that it imposes on the rest of the world the creative force, spiritual complexity, and intellectual sophistication of various cultures and histories that have emerged in Africa and that continue to evolve, transform, and delight millions of people who are living day-to-day in those worlds.

This year's box set continues the work of expanding our opportunity to read writers from areas of Africa that have not been as well-represented in the previous box sets. Two of our poets, Hazem Fahmy and Rabha Ashry, are Egyptians, though the latter was born in Abu Dhabi. We are publishing our first Rwandan poet, Alain Jules Hirwa, and it is good to have Botswanan poet Phodiso Modirwa featured in this box set. Nigeria continues to produce poets of varied styles and themes, and four of them, Samuel Adeyemi, O-Jeremiah Agbaakin, Nneoma Veronica Nwogu, and Jakky Bankong-Obi, are featured in this box set. Three poets from Ghana are featured here, as well: Jay Kophy, Tawiah Mensah, and Nikitta Dede Adjirakor.

We remain deeply moved by the quality of work that we see in this process year after year. The eleven poets included here were drawn from about forty-eight solicited manuscripts that we received this year, based on recommendations from our community of poets, critics, and arts organizers. We have continued to pay attention to poets whose work has appeared in journals and other forums, and we have also relied on poets whose work has emerged in our various contests. We continue to look for ways to ensure that we are reaching more poetry communities around Africa, and our hope is to continue to provide a platform for these poets through our various projects.

—Kwame Dawes

Part Two

My desire to assist in developing a living archive is a deep and abiding one. Living archives are seen as part of the praxis of social (in this case, artistic as well) memory and transmission. We can say for instance that a living archive refers to practices and conditions, even environments, that connect curation to transmission that is performative, participatory, and always creative. By its very nature, it is community bound and based and must be reflexive in real time.

Growing up as a young reader and writer in West Africa, I was privileged to have access to several book series. The famous Heinemann African Writers Series, edited by Chinua Achebe and later by Abdulrazak Gurnah, was an incredibly robust and important series that was published from 1962 up through the early 2000s. Almost every writer who makes up the first modern wave of African Writers, three who went on to win Nobel Prizes, including Abdulrazak, were first published in the Heinemann series. The writers hailed from Egypt to South Africa, from the Eastern coast to the West, and all the points within. The series focused mostly on fiction but the occasional poet made the cut, and we have republished several of those in our own series. The Heinemann series was over five hundred books long. No small thing.

Then there was the Pacesetter Series by Macmillan. It was a series of novellas, but with the scope of full novels, that focused on genre fiction for young adults. This series inspired my first book, *Masters of the Board*. They had about one hundred titles.

The third series was by Longman, and it was aimed squarely at college and high school course adoption. They curated a lot of post-Civil War books, and many of the historical and social works around this rupture in Nigeria's history were published there.

There were a few other local publishers taking stabs at this time, though they didn't run specific series and had varied editorial lists. Notably Fagbamigbe Publishing, whose star writer, Louis Omotayo Johnson, sold nearly a hundred thousand copies of his detective series books, which in '90s Nigeria was nothing short of a miracle. Then there was Spectrum, who didn't really rise to any real intervention because they were caught between a desire for trade publishing and the rarified air of textbook publishing. Finally, of note, was Delta, run by Nigerian writer Dillibe Onyeama. Delta published my first novel.

There are several things you may notice here. First is that Nigeria and Nigerians get mentioned a lot. This isn't because of any chauvinism on my part, but simply because with the biggest population on the continent, and one of the most vibrant and successful economies, Nigeria exerts an overly large impact on all areas of continental life. In fact, Nobel Prize Winner Nadine Gordimer of South Africa is quoted as saying that 70 percent of African literature is Nigerian literature. This is not to say there weren't interventions in other countries—Weaver Press from Zimbabwe is a notable one, and there were many from South Africa. I am speaking, however, of curated and enduring series. The second thing you may notice is that these series seldom include any poetry or poets, which is what makes what we do unique, important, and bearing the weight of many years of urgency.

You may wonder why you are getting this history lesson. There are multiple reasons. The first is that for a writer to combat the crushing weight of western literary hegemonies, an accessible tradition and an archive of that tradition is needed beyond what words can express. To find innovation, tradition, and the span of history within a literary culture that is DNA-deep is an incredible opportunity.

Then there are the three main parts of a living archive that keep it relevant and ever expanding (outside of the constant drive for funds and publishing partnerships) and these are:

1. The Historical Narrative: With time this builds itself, but with careful planning we have started to draw books and writers back into print from the periods covered by initial series and archives, with the hope of sustaining this, giving as big a historical narrative span backward and forward in time as we can. And we hope to hand this off soon to a new generation.
2. Current Reelections and Planning: We see through these introductions the conversations that develop across and between books and poets, and how these shape and drive the content of the work. It allows us to see what the current conversations are and how best to curate and organize.
3. Real Time Feedback: We can pivot, change, expand, and open more curatorial, editorial, and publishing spaces based on the feedback from all work that is submitted to us, including any work we publish. And based on the work we review, we can look at what education and training could be useful.

Where all the other series that I spoke of were by foreign companies and publishing endeavors, ours is fully African-driven and not owned for profit. We plan for an ongoing home for contemporary African poetry, and with time we hope to find ourselves in a place where we can purchase and reintroduce the series from Heinemann, Longman, and Macmillan.

In just over eight years, we have published over 100 hundred chapbooks, and if we include the larger parts of the African Poetry Book Fund, that's about 150 writers. It seems a lot, but this is nothing given the size of the talent pool on the continent. It is at best a calling card. We hope to partner on the continent with more publishing collectives and endeavors so that the archive will grow, becoming so decentralized that it can never die. A living archive for the ages.

—Chris Abani

The Chapbooks of
Tisa: New-Generation African Poets, A Chapbook Box Set

At the Gates by Hazem Fahmy
with a preface by Danusha Laméris

Grief and Ecstasy by Rabha Ashry
with a preface by Malika Booker

Hairpins by Alain Jules Hirwa
with a preface by Thabile Makue

here, there, and what is broken in between
by Nneoma Veronica Nwogu
with a preface by Saddiq Dzukogi

Learning to Say My Name by Nikitta Dede Adjirakor
with a preface by Victoria Adukwei Bulley

A Litany on Loss by Tawiah Naana Akua Mensah
with a preface by Matthew Shenoda

Maceration by Jay Kophy
with a preface by Therí Alyce Pickens

Rose Ash by Samuel A. Adeyemi
with a preface by Patricia Jabbeh Wesley

The Sign of the Ram by O-Jeremiah Agbaakin
with a preface by 'Gbenga Adeoba

Speaking in Code by Phodiso Modirwa
with a preface by Tsitsi Jaji

What Still Yields by Jakky Bankong-Obi
with a preface by Mahtem Shiferraw

INTRODUCTION TO
KUMI: NEW-GENERATION AFRICAN POETS,
A CHAPBOOK BOX SET
2024

Featured poets: Adams Adeosun, Feranmi Ariyo, Sarpong Osei Asamoah, Connor Cogill, Nurain Ọládèjì, Claudia Owusu, Nome Emeka Patrick, Dare Tunmise, Qhali

Featured artist: Kokeb Zeleke

Introduction in Two Movements

Part One

The singular lesson I have learned in the nearly ten years of editing these box sets and other projects for the African Poetry Book Fund is quite simple—gratitude. Gratitude is at the very core of Igbo and Yoruba worldviews. When you ask someone how they are in a casual greeting, they often reply: "I remain grateful." For me, gratitude is a practical matter and is, in this case, linked to foundations, community, and witness.

There is the remarkable foundation of the APBF—from the planning, vision, and ethics that went into its inception, the earlier models it was built on, and the serendipitous meeting of capital and potential, to the deep generosity of financial, publishing, and editorial partnerships. There are many reasons why APBF should not exist, but it does, and it continues to thrive and flourish. Gratitude.

The community that this convergence has generated is amazing: there is the volunteer-run editorial board comprising some of the most awarded and respected African poets of our time; the volunteer staff who support the work, many of them poets on the cusp of breaking out in their own careers; and the poets themselves, who have gone on to publish full-length books, to flourish in graduate programs, to support emerging poets and each other, and to steer others to this unique home we have built. Gratitude.

To continue to be able to edit and offer these books. To witness a thriving and flourishing aesthetic emergence in poetry—perhaps the largest and most diverse by nation, border, and identity—arising from the continent and its diaspora to date. To witness an explosion of work that will continue to grow and flourish long after Kwame and I hand over the project to the next generation. Gratitude.

Not all of these poets have MFAs or workshop experience; several of them emerged through community efforts and self-education. Yet these voices are nonetheless assured and mature. Often referring to other chapbooks in the series, these writers learn from *each other*. This is something we have seen evolve in intertextuality, conversations across crafts, subject matter, and even political concerns—we also see these as conversations on how to make poetry.

Adams Adeosun's chapbook *If the Golden Hour Won't Come for Us* begins with these lines:

> And above all, I desire cleanness,
>   baptism more than a scrubbing down,
>
> an animal softer than my body

It's a bold invitation to reclamation. It's prayer in its best form, a sort of blasphemy, and a negotiation with forces larger than oneself. In a way, it embodies the heart of the reggae aesthetic, which is simultaneously lamentation, social justice demand, and the sensuality of life. A form of gratitude, nonetheless.

In his chapbook *Light Through Water*, Cape Town poet Connor Cogill writes:

This home has been
in our family for generations. I will not ask
whose war. I will not ask whose land. I will
tell a charming story: how I was born
("Continent without a name")

Here we are invited into a self-implicating conversation about race within Africa—something not often addressed in conquest and colonialism—and a generation made collateral, both on the terms of the colonized and the colonizer.

Feranmi Ariyo's *I Watch You Disappear* offers ritual and internment of smoke in "The Last Smoke." He writes: "And once, after we learn he is never going to recover, / my soon-to-be-dead father asks for a cigarette." There is this constant attendance to the personal, the political, the communal—an engagement wrestling with the shapes, challenges, and pressures of being human. There are attempted negotiations with guilt, with lineage, with culpability, and much more. A true representation of the fact of one of my claims, which is that African writers are the curators of Africa's humanity.

Claudia Owusu's chapbook *In These Bones, I Am Shifting* explores the relationship of the body to shame, sacrifice, and complicity, though one belied by a collective hope. In these we find again the power of transformation, transubstantiation even, or one can say, a restatement of reclamation. Here water, which has been undergirding all the books in this box set, reveals the power to transform. In "Drown or Drought" she writes:

> In Taifa, my pee-stained bed sheets hung out on the line for the world to see.
> My cousins, siblings, and I spent the school break waiting for rain

I find myself unintentionally following water in this box set, as lineage, as ablution, as hope, as an uncompromising restitution, and as a thread. As editors we don't assign themes for the box sets, and we don't frame the call in this way either. But somehow, a dominant theme emerges, as though a collective unconscious has been formed. Gratitude.

In the chapbook *Crying in My Mother's Tongue*, South African poet Qhali writes:

> i found it above me on a tree and asked it why They didn't take me when i went in
> it got up and flew away   i followed it   umama told the psychiatrist
> ("the water returns to you")

This echoes the great Bessie Head, another South African writer, who struggled with a similar legacy. We see this most starkly in Head's *A Question of Power*, where she writes a kind of terrifying love, a kind of brokenness that is more whole than wholeness and attempts to negotiate with the legacies of the trauma of apartheid and the continent's oppression. This impossible math, which is a kind of hope, runs through these chapbooks:

> Before the consecration,
> I was a light lost in my mother's womb
> —"Inheritance"
> *A Failed Attempt at Undoing Memories* by Dare Tunmise

Or when Nome Emeka Patrick writes in the poem "A Midnight Storm, Outside the Wild" from the chapbook *Voyaging*:

> The night is a wet grave. I'm in a room whose dark has eyes.

In the hands of less mature writers, these themes and subthemes, couched in such language, would be sentimental or disturbing. In the hands of these writers, they are disruptive but redemptive too.

Sarpong Osei Asamoah in *Yaanom* and the poem "Testimony" continues the thread unspooling throughout all these chapbooks:

> In my mother's garden, there's a bioluminescent wound in
>   the loam
> through which God spies on the world.
> I am the door.

And to bring the journey to an end, but also to restart it—here is Nurain Qládèjì in "Facing East," a poem from his chapbook *Home is a Heart That Flees*:

> I turn to face east; everywhere else leads away
> from truth. I know because I followed each road

> Follow the road, the thread, and the flow of water and words to the end of this offering and experience gratitude with me.

> —*Chris Abani*

Part Two

> "Modernity is not always the answer,
> sometimes antiquity is, too."
> —*The Crown*

> "Elegies are one of the few places where we can do the work of care, not just to ourselves but to our dead..."
> —Romeo Oriogun

When we began this box set series, Chris Abani and I agreed to produce a set every year and that upon completing the tenth we would review the series and see what the steady and consistent gathering of new African voices in poetry offered. I believe we made a prudent decision, born of our circumstances, to refrain from dictating a direction for the poetry that we would solicit. Fully aware that despite our intentions, the fact that we were making our decisions around a set of values based on what we felt was poetry with vision, clarity, coherent and consistent ambition, and venturesomeness, each box set would send a message to emerging poets that could seem didactic.

Rather than proceed to shape a poetics for the series, we decided to suppress this instinct and replace it with consideration for the collective weight of the sixty to seventy manuscripts that came to us from all around the continent and her diaspora, as evidence of the state of poetry on the continent. We sought to be guided by what we were seeing, to test it all, and report on what we had seen. Abani's introduction to this box set is a brilliant, generous, and aptly exciting reporting of what we have seen and witnessed in these manuscripts. Abani has shown us that one of the most promising qualities emerging in these ten years of chapbooks, totaling more than a hundred poets, is the simple but meaningful fact that these poets are in conversation. They are reading each other because they have access to each other's writing. They are forming distinctive poetic visions, finding the points of connection between themselves as poets and their necessary differences. In some cases, these poets may know each other, but for the most part, they are meeting each other through their poems.

In many ways, these writers, consciously or unconsciously feeding each other, are pushing against a recent critique of contemporary African poetry that worried the work is imitative and derivative of non-African poetry. Superficially, there is evidence to support this claim. Phrases like "exit wounds" and titles that declare the poems as "self-portraits," as well as an inordinate number of "erasure" poems, "duplexes," and contrapuntal poems appear with faddish regularity. Yet in the best work, these are often borrowed suits trying and failing to contain the bodies of the poems emerging. Of course, there is no sin in this kind of imitation and dialogue. Rather than lament the influence of the West on African poetry, it is becoming increasingly clear that African poets are bringing new obsessions and preoccupations to poetry.

Put another way, the years of relative silence of African poets in print, not only on the world stage but in African countries across generations, has meant that poets writing today have a double gift: the exciting prospect of being chroniclers of their moment in a rapidly transforming world, and the feeling that they are serving as the first correspondents of their world, their landscape, and their particular cultural space. It is easy and wrong to overstate this role. For though it is factual to say that the publication of African poetry has been in the doldrums for many years, it is equally factual to say that African poetry in all its remarkable manifestations has never waned, but has thrived—as a powerful fact of the life of Africans in song, griot speak, proverbs, indigenous poetic cycles, and ubiquitous performances throughout African cultures.

We have seen a splendid proliferation of African poetry in print doing the hard and necessary work of chronicling the sentiment of our time. Abani has made the phrase "a living archive" a central source of purpose and intentionality for this series and the other publishing ventures we have undertaken in African poetry. It is this that allows us to accept some of the limitations of our series. As many have discovered, our print runs are modest and some editions can now safely be called collectors' items. We are also aware that our distribution in Africa is limited by circumstances we can't control, though we are making great efforts to improve this. But we take comfort in the fact that these poets are in print, accessible, and creating a body of work. Our last edition, *TISA*, has been especially successful, featured on multiple best-of lists.

This is our tenth edition of the *New-Generation African Poets* series, and we remain committed to our partnership with Akashic Books and our friends and informal advisors around the world who send us recommendations of African poets to whom we ought to pay attention. This edition, as Abani eloquently points out, is a stunning body of truly exciting contemporary African poetry. Varied, accomplished, eclectic, wholly alive, and wonderfully revelatory of how younger African poets are writing nations and selves in these times.

In this gathering, there is a refreshing sense of the immediate and the future, but, and for me more critically, there is also a growing engagement with the past, with antiquity and tradition, with the bold and healing acknowledgment of the value of our past as Africans, of our ancestors and the legacy of this continent's power and beauty, qualities that have been threatened often by the ugliness of colonialism and imperialism.

We can say with great confidence that the present and future of African poetry is in very good hands.

—Kwame Dawes

The Chapbooks of
Kumi: New-Generation African Poets, A Chapbook Box Set

Crying in My Mother's Tongue by Qhali
with a preface by Safia Elhillo

A Failed Attempt at Undoing Memories by Dare Tunmise
with a preface by Tjawangwa Dema

Home Is a Heart That Flees by Nurain Ọládèjì
with a preface by Tyree Daye

If the Golden Hour Won't Come for Us by Adams Adeosun
with a preface by Mahtem Shiferraw

In These Bones, I Am Shifting by Claudia Owusu
with a preface by Sherry Shenoda

I Watch You Disappear by Feranmi Ariyo
with a preface by Saddiq Dzukogi

Light Through Water by Connor Cogill
with a preface by Uhuru Phalafala

Voyaging by Nome Emeka Patrick
with a preface by Matthew Shenoda

Yaanom by Sarpong Osei Asamoah
with a preface by Kwame Dawes

Lorna Dawes

KWAME DAWES is the author of numerous books of poetry and other works of fiction, criticism, and essays. His most recent poetry collection, *Sturge Town*, was published by Peepal Tree Press in the UK and W. W. Norton in the US. Dawes is a professor of Literary Arts at Brown University. He also teaches in the Pacific MFA Program and is the series editor of the African Poetry Book Series, director of the African Poetry Book Fund, and artistic director of the Calabash International Literary Festival. He is a Chancellor for the Academy of American Poets and a Fellow of the Royal Society of Literature. Dawes is the winner of the prestigious Windham-Campbell Prize for Poetry and was a finalist for the 2022 Neustadt International Prize for Literature. In 2022, Kwame Dawes was awarded the Order of Distinction Commander Class by the Government of Jamaica, and in 2024, he was appointed Poet Laureate of Jamaica.

Chris Abani

CHRIS ABANI's prose includes *The Secret History of Las Vegas*, *Song for Night*, *The Virgin of Flames*, *Becoming Abigail*, *GraceLand*, and *Masters of the Board*. His poetry collections include *Smoking the Bible*, *Sanctificum*, *There Are No Names for Red*, *Feed Me the Sun*, *Hands Washing Water*, *Dog Woman*, *Daphne's Lot*, and *Kalakuta Republic*. He holds a BA and MA in English, an MA in gender and culture, and a PhD in literature and creative writing. Abani is the recipient of a PEN America Freedom to Write Award, a Prince Claus Award, a Lannan Literary fellowship, a California Book Award, a Hurston/Wright Legacy Award, a PEN Beyond Margins Award, a PEN/Hemingway Award, and a Guggenheim fellowship. He won the prestigious 2024 UNT Rilke Prize and was a finalist for the 2024 Neustadt International Prize for Literature. He is also a member of the American Academy of Arts and Sciences. Born in Nigeria, he is currently on the board of trustees, a professor of English, and director of African Studies at Northwestern University.

Ae Hee Lee

SIWAR MASANNAT is a Jordanian writer and the author of *cue* (Georgia Review Books/University of Georgia Press, 2024) and *50 Water Dreams* (Cleveland State University Poetry Center, 2015). Masannat holds a PhD in English from the University of Wisconsin in Milwaukee, an MFA from George Mason University, and a BSc from the University of Jordan. Masannat works as Assistant Director of the African Poetry Book Fund and teaches at Brown University.

Also available from Akashic Books and the African Poetry Book Fund

Eight New-Generation African Poets: A Chapbook Box Set
ISBN: 978-1-61775-355-8| $29.95

Featured poets: Peter Akinlabi, Viola Allo, Inua Ellams, Liyou Libsekal, Amy M. Lukau, Vuyelwa Maluleke, Blessing Musariri, Janet Kofi-Tsekpo

Tatu: New-Generation African Poets, A Chapbook Box Set
ISBN: 978-1-61775-451-7| $29.95

Featured poets: D.M. Aderibigbe, Gbenga Adesina, Kayombo Chingonyi, Safia Elhillo, Chielozona Eze, Nyachiro Lydia Kasese, Ngwatilo Mawiyoo, Hope Wabuke

Nne: New-Generation African Poets, A Chapbook Box Set
ISBN: 978-1-617755-540-8 | $29.95

Featured poets: Yasmin Belkhyr, Victoria Adukwei Bulley, Mary-Alice Daniel, Chekwube O. Danladi, Lena Bezawork Grönlund, Ashley Makue, Momtaza Mehri, Famia Nkansa, Ejiọfọr Ugwu, Chimwemwe Undi

Tano: New-Generation African Poets, A Chapbook Box Set
ISBN: 978-1-61775-623-8 | $34.95

Featured poets: Leila Chatti, Saddiq Dzukogi, Amanda Bintu Holiday, Omotara James, Yalie Kamara, Rasaq Malik, Umniya Najaer, Kechi Nomu, Romeo Oriogun, Henk Rossouw, Alexis Teyie

Sita: New-Generation African Poets, A Chapbook Box Set
ISBN: 978-1-61775-717-4 | $34.95

Featured poets: 'Gbenga Adeoba, Hiwot Adilow, Dina El Dessouky, Ama Asantewa Diaka, Dalia Elhassan, Charity Hutete, Nour Kamel, Musawenkosi Khanyile, Daisy Odey, Salawu Olajide

Saba: New-Generation African Poets, A Chapbook Box Set
ISBN: 978-1-61775-816-4 | $34.95

Featured poets: Adedayo Adeyemi Agarau, Michelle K. Angwenyi, Afua Ansong, Fatima Camara, Sadia Hassan, Safia Jama, Henneh Kyereh Kwaku, Nadra Mabrouk, Nkateko Masinga, Jamila Osman, Tryphena Yeboah

Nane: New-Generation African Poets, A Chapbook Box Set
ISBN: 978-1-61775-950-5 | $34.95

Featured poets: Kolawole Samuel Adebayo, Cynthia Amoah, Precious Arinze, Lameese Badr, Sara Elkamel, Edil Hassan, Jeremy Teddy Karn, Hauwa Shaffii Nuhu, Selina Nwulu, Ayan M. Omar, Saradha Soobrayen, Ajibola Tolase, Qutouf Yahia

Tisa: New-Generation African Poets, A Chapbook Box Set
ISBN: 978-1-63614-076-6 | $36.95

Featured poets: Samuel A. Adeyemi, Nikitta Dede Adjirakor, O-Jeremiah Agbaakin, Rabha Ashry, Hazem Fahmy, Alain Jules Hirwa, Jay Kophy, Tawiah Naana Akua Mensah, Phodiso Modirwa, Nneoma Veronica Nwogu, Jakky Bankong-Obi

Kumi: New-Generation African Poets, A Chapbook Box Set
ISBN: 978-1-63614-188-6 | $36.95

Featured poets: Adams Adeosun, Feranmi Ariyo, Sarpong Osei Asamoah, Connor Cogill, Nurain Ọládèjì, Claudia Owusu, Nome Emeka Patrick, Dare Tunmise, Qhali

Kumi Na Moja: New-Generation African Poets, A Chapbook Box Set
Forthcoming, December 2025, ISBN: 978-1-63614-241-8 | $40

Featured Poets: Abdulkareem Abdulkareem, Hauwa Saleh Abubakar, Aria Deemie, Michael Imossan, Rahma Jimoh, Roseline Mgbodichinma, Adesiyan Oluwapelumi, Leano Debra Ranko, Timi Sanni, and Tjizembua Tjikuzu

Available from our website and wherever books are sold
www.akashicbooks.com | info@akashicbooks.com